Dear Teenage Girl:

You're Already Amazing!

A Simple and Powerful Guide to Discovering Self-Worth, Cultivating Healthy Relationships, and Building Self-Confidence

PUBLISHED BY: Shannon Cooke

Table of Contents

Introduction

Everything you want to be, you already are. You're simply on the path to discovering it. –Alicia Keys

Human beings are constantly evolving into more of themselves, and too often, it isn't until adulthood that they begin to really dive into what's going on in their minds and bodies. I mean, have you ever really looked at yourself in the mirror— full-length mirror, vulnerable and raw—and really saw yourself? Have you seen not only the beautiful body that carries you but also your true being through your eyes without the voice of society or other people in the back of your mind tricking you into critiquing yourself rather than admiring the miracle?

If you have done this before, I applaud you and hope that you continue to notice the wonderful things that make you special. If you haven't, that is the very first thing I invite you to try. It requires nothing other than a mirror, privacy, and courage— the courage to embrace yourself and to discover that you have the power to do and be anything you wish, along with the never-ending choice to change as many times as you want. Begin by choosing a time in which you won't be interrupted

4

and stand in front of a mirror. Scan your body, admiring how it bends and folds. Then, look into your eyes, arms resting by your sides or holding yourself lightly, and repeat the following words:

I am open and ready to learn.

I am loved.

My value does not decrease based on other people's opinions.

I belong.

I am capable.

In a world in which the media pushes ideal body types using filters that don't represent reality, having a body is hard. If you feel this way, it's not because you are doing anything wrong; it is simply because you are human. Imagine the power that could come from this simple practice of self-reflection. We have the ability to believe anything we want. The key is to choose to train ourselves to live and act from love. This book is written for teenage girls who feel unseen, for those who struggle with confidence, for those who don't ever feel like they are doing the right thing. You are enough, no matter what people say or how many mistakes you may make, no matter what you look like, no matter your mood, interests, or grades. You are enough just as you are. With the use of exercises like the one above, reflections, and research-presented facts, this book will provide you with the skills and confidence to go out into the world independent and living with self-awareness and universal connection.

I am sure you have seen a yin-yang symbol. This symbol represents harmony and balance: light within the darkness and darkness within the light. In life, you cannot know success if you do not also experience failure, just as you cannot know happiness if you do not also experience sadness. The key is to embrace the ebb and flow of life, knowing that you remain in control of the way you react to its changes. While the teen years will always be filled with highs, lows, and brief glimpses of steadiness, they don't have to be compounded by low self-esteem, unsureness, and unreachable expectations. The aim of this book is to offer knowledge of the human mind and body and to provide guidance to be truly and completely yourself, loving and embracing flaws and all.

The ability to listen to your body, own a sense of pride, know your worth, and learn how to handle peer pressure can make your teen years so much more enjoyable and less fearful. Every day, month, and year is made up of billions of tiny moments that shape and challenge our minds and enable us to learn more about what we like and what we don't, what kind of people we feel the most relaxed around, and the traits we find less desirable in ourselves and others. This book teaches you how to train your brain to recognize more moments of joy among the chaos.

Teens are rapidly evolving mentally, emotionally, and physically all while navigating puberty, personal hygiene, school, relationships, family, and societal expectations. That is a lot to handle, especially when you are still learning about yourself. As a teen girl who grew up shy and unsure, I confess that I struggled hard to find myself and feel confident in my life, to embrace my body and every inch of my soul. It used to sound impossible to me. I never believed I would love myself or that anyone else would see any value in me, but then I went through a few life experiences that inspired me to explore the self-help genre, and here I am today, finally loving life and eager to inspire teenage girls to start the journey to self-acceptance and love way sooner than I did.

This book is written for teen Shannon, for my daughters, granddaughters, and all teen girls who can't yet see their worth, who can't yet see how their amazing presence positively influences those who come across their path. This is for the girls who exude confidence but don't actually feel it, for the girls who sit at the back of the class and avoid making eye-contact, for the girls who try their hardest to get good grades and for the girls who are just getting by, for the girls who try to get from home to school in one piece, and for those who stand tall and those who hide in the shadows.

This book is for any girl struggling to fit in. For any girl who wants to learn more about herself, analyze her relationships, give energy to those who praise her, and let go of those who hold her down. For the girl who wants to grow her confidence from the inside out and learn how to live mindfully, aware of your thought patterns and triggers. Learn ways to challenge and change your thinking by remaining open-minded. Learn from those who fall and choose to rise again and again.

I challenge you to read this book from cover to cover and see firsthand how changing your mindset can change your life. Your mind will believe whatever story you tell it, so take charge and tell a great story.

Chapter 1: Conscious Versus Subconscious Mind

No problem can be solved from the same level of consciousness that created it. –Albert Einstein

The above quote is not to say that a person cannot solve their own problems; rather, in order to see a solution, one must first elevate their consciousness. One must gain a new way of thinking.

The mind is a powerful thing, and it is important to remember that though people can and do have control over their thoughts and actions, your age predicts the brain's ability to control emotional reactions. Teen brains are still developing; thus they are more likely than adults to react emotionally and perhaps irrationally. Thinking before you act is a learned skill, and let's be real, a lot of adults have yet to master it, but it is something that can be controlled as you gain more awareness of self and others. This chapter is not to place blame or to remove it from any action but to encourage you to understand that the teen brain is under construction, and the way you train your mind is a vital element to living a fulfilling and enjoyable life.

Perfection does not exist. Attempting to attain something that is unreachable is only going to deteriorate your mental and physical health. Evolving the way we think, what we think about, and the quality of our thoughts is something everyone has to do for themselves. Whether you worry about your intelligence, future, or past, your ambitions, appearance, or likeability, you have the power to train your mind and to choose to change your self- and world-perception. This chapter will guide you through cultivating awareness via the power of thought and of self-talk. Following and reflecting on the information shared will help you to know yourself on a deeper level and provide tools to use to process change with a more stable mind.

While we all view the world through our own lens, seeking love, connection, and belonging is a natural part of being human. Emotions are not unique to the individual; rather, they are part of the collective human experience. Our personal nature, as well as our nurture or the way we were raised, along with life experiences and what we are exposed to all contribute to our understanding of the world around us and how we see ourselves.

The conscious part of the mind is responsible for logical thinking and rationalizing, whereas the subconscious part of the mind is responsible for involuntary actions. You don't think about how to breathe; you just do it. This is your subconscious mind in action. You can, however, consciously control the breath and the length and depth of each inhale and exhale; this is your conscious mind in action.

The remainder of this chapter explores the conscious and subconscious mind. You may not have control over everything that happens in your life, but you can develop a kind, compassionate relationship with yourself by learning how to notice and choose your inner voice. This will enable you to better navigate the ever-changing aspects of life as you go through school, relationships, physical changes, and so much more.

The Conscious Mind

I want people to walk around delusional about how great they can be - and then to fight so hard for it every day that the lie becomes the truth.

–Lady Gaga

Fitting in Versus Belonging, Cora's Story

Cora was a 15-year-old girl who had yet to feel like she belonged anywhere, was desperate to be liked, and was always scrambling within her mind to make friends and find a place she felt like herself. But Cora wasn't sure what she liked because she was so focused on fitting in that she made choices based on what the people around her were doing. Her childhood friend had moved to a different school and had new friends who invited her to join the volleyball team. Cora took up volleyball when she heard of this, but she wasn't very good and didn't make any of the teams she tried out for. Her parents were busy with work or with her younger brother at the hockey rink. Cora tried to sell hot chocolate at the canteen, but after a few kids burned their tongues, she had to stop. At school, Cora received decent grades and excelled in the arts like sculpting, music, and drama, but none of her friends were into that stuff, so she changed her interests, hobbies, and even the way she spoke all in the hopes of finding a sense of belonging.

Cora was very good at putting on any mask necessary to fit in with those around her. However, at night when she would lie in bed, she still had a feeling of loneliness. Anyone on the outside viewing Cora's life would say she was a well-rounded girl capable of fitting in anywhere. Why didn't Cora feel this way? She tried for years to fill the space within that always felt empty, and it wasn't until her senior year of high school that she decided to stop trying to fit in and to just do what she was interested in.

When one of Cora's classmates invited her to ultimate Frisbee tryouts, for the first time in Cora's life, she said, "No, thanks. I'm going to try out for the choir." Cora didn't know anyone who was in the choir and walked into tryouts feeling very nervous, but she was determined to do something she wanted to do. Before she finished her audition, people were clapping and congratulating her on joining the choir. Cora was invited to join the choir kids for lunch and to practice in the stairwells during breaks, and she did. For the first time, Cora was able to just be herself, to sing with other people who liked music as much as she did. Cora found people she could relate to, people with whom she could be relaxed and accepted without having to put on any sort of show or mask to fit in.

Cora's story describes what so many people choose to do in life: to be what they think others want them to be before figuring out who they want themselves to be. In her book, *Braving the Wilderness*, author Brene Brown describes fitting in and belonging as follows (Brown, 2019):

"Belonging is being accepted for you. Fitting in is being accepted for being like everyone else. If I get to be me, I belong. If I have to be like you, I fit in."

Cora found a sense of desire to be herself and to do what made her happy. When she finally put herself first, she found contentment. She lost some old friends while others were happy she found a passion of her own. As difficult as it is to choose to take a risk and go out on your own instead of doing what you think others expect, it is worth facing this fear, because what you find on the other side is inexplicable to those who have yet to experience the freedom of self-expression and self-acceptance.

Building Self-Awareness

One of the many things my parents taught me, and I'll always be grateful for the gift, is to not ever let anybody else define me.

–Wilma Mankiller

You are capable of narrating your own life, changing the plot, and adding unexpected twists and turns, adventure and excitement, and sorrow and loss. Sure, other people can tell you what they'd like you to do. They may only speak of their interests and rarely ask about yours, but the only way they control you is if you allow them to. Words can and do hurt, but we have the power to define ourselves when we tap into our levels of consciousness and learn who we are at the core of our being.

Cora's story demonstrates what has been described by Brene Brown as noticing the difference between fitting in and feeling a genuine sense of belonging.

Your conscious mind is comprised of the following attributes:

- self-awareness

- thoughts

- feelings

- perceptions

- sensations

- memories

- fantasies

Anything within your current awareness, thoughts, feelings, and environment is consciousness. It is not possible for the mind to recall every experience, thought, or feeling at all times, so what is not needed immediately in the current environment is stored but still accessible. You can remember stories of your childhood, and while they are part of your conscious mind, you do not think about them every moment of the day. They are stored in the preconscious mind. Imagine an iceberg; your consciousness is the part above the water and your preconsciousness is the part just below the surface (Cherry, 2006).

As the brain continues to develop into young adulthood, you learn how to respond to various challenges, changes, and experiences in a way to help yourself thrive. Along the way, you will make mistakes, you will lose, and you will feel sadness and embarrassment, but through all of this you will flourish as a young adult gaining knowledge that enables you to navigate the world with self-awareness and confidence. The prefrontal cortex, or the part of the brain behind your forehead, is not thought to be fully developed until the age of 25. This is the part of the brain responsible for controlling impulses. It enables you to plan and organize your behavior in order to meet a goal, so it is natural that people react impulsively or in irrational ways prior to the age of 25. This, however, is not to be used as an excuse for poor behavior choices resulting in negative consequences (Cox, 2011).

Increased awareness of thought patterns and your inner voice allows you to change the quality of your thoughts, essentially meaning that you can create your perception of reality if you work at it. Noticing the tone your voice takes when perceiving yourself and others is the first step to accepting your true self and allowing your light to shine brightly with less hesitation.

Below, you will find a list of reflection prompts to help you notice your mind with more detail. You may choose to write or draw your thoughts and feelings in your own journal, or perhaps you'll imagine them without moving a muscle. Regardless of your experience with these reflections, they will increase your self-awareness. There is no order in which to reflect on these prompts. Do one now and continue through the chapter, coming back later. Perhaps you'd like to do more than one or to do them all at once. No matter your method, this is an invitation to explore your consciousness.

- What would you title this stage of your life right now?

    o Why do you think this title fits?

- When, where, and with whom do you feel the most at ease being yourself?

    o Describe the environment in which you feel the most calm.

- What are the characteristics of the people around whom you feel content and free?

- If you could tell a family member, friend, or partner any three things without worry of their reaction, what would you say?

  - Imagine the person or people you want to speak with.

  - Notice the first three things that come to mind but ponder as many as necessary.

  - Imagine saying those things to someone. What feelings come up for you? Why have you chosen not to share this information?

- Describe yourself with a minimum of five words.

  - Which category do the words fall under? (character, intelligence, ability, appearance, possessions, mannerisms, feelings)

  - Have these words been spoken to you before? By whom? Why or why not?

  - How many of the words you have chosen are positive or negative?

- What makes you happy?

  - Can you make more time in your life for what makes you happy?

- Which five words do you want other people to use to describe you?

    ○ Write these words and leave them by your bed to read each night and day.

    ○ Say these words to yourself while looking in a mirror at least once a day.

    ○ Whether you believe these words or not, the power of saying them can train your conscience to believe them to be true.

Confidence doesn't always come with ease, but it exists within you already. Your job is to bring it into your reality. The more you examine your thoughts, their origins, and their impacts on the mind, body, and relationships, the more you will understand feelings that arise and the better you will be equipped to respond in a manner that will help you. Imagine the life you want to live and tell yourself that it is achievable, or pretend you already have it. "Fake it til you make it" isn't a common phrase for no reason. There is power in thought.

Create the truth you desire by using language that supports what you want. For example, if you fail a project or test, it is normal to feel defeated, and you can find a way to move forward within the disappointment by changing the narrative. Remember, light exists within the dark, and dark exists within the light. Instead of, "I'm so stupid. I didn't study hard enough. I am so embarrassed," change your perspective by asking yourself, "What factors contributed to this outcome? Was I tired or hungry? Did I fight with my friend or family member? Was I more focused on a sporting or arts event than studying? Do I need to ask for clarification?" Going further, say to yourself, "I am capable. I can learn and improve. My worth does not decrease based on a test result or someone's inability to see my light. I am human."

Some of you reading this may think that the above suggestion sounds ridiculous, time-consuming, or even irritating. When I was 24 and experiencing bouts of depression in which I battled with my mind on a regular basis, someone told me to look in the mirror more often and change my negative thoughts to positive ones. When you're deep in the dark, someone saying, "Just think positive," is enough to make you want to rage out, but you don't, because your conscious brain knows it is not beneficial.

I started by writing affirmations on the fogged-up bathroom mirror when I was finished in the shower. "I am beautiful. I am worthy. I am enough. I will get through this." Sometimes, I would feel frustrated or dumb and would either not write anything or immediately wipe it off so no one would see, but I told myself I would do it just so I could at least say, "See? Nothing works. The dark has swallowed me whole."

I will not promise you that this practice of changing how you speak to and about yourself will work immediately, but I can attest to my experience that over time, you will notice that you think those words and that the negative thoughts will slowly be replaced or at least quieted. This is the process of linking the conscience with the subconscious. Train your mind.

The Subconscious Mind

I think women want freedom. They want to be empowered. They want hope. They want love. –Rihanna

The subconscious mind is the part of the iceberg that is deep below the surface of the water. It is always on, always working, storing, sorting, and choosing which information you have access to. When you are awake, you are conscious, and when you go to sleep, so does your consciousness. However, your subconscious never sleeps. It is constantly taking in information and creating your dreams and often dictating your self-perception from your memories, feelings, and desires (Peer, 2019).

Have you ever had an overwhelming feeling take over your mind and body seemingly out of the blue without being able to pinpoint where it came from? Do you have a fear of something but cannot remember why it gives you the heebie-jeebies? Have you reacted to something someone else viewed as small that you felt was a big deal? If so, congratulations, you are in fact a human being! The subconscious stores everything that we have ever experienced, and sometimes the stories it holds impact our actions, reactions, understandings, and emotions without us being aware of it. One key to linking the conscious and subconscious mind is by self-reflection. The more we understand ourselves, the more level-headed we are when conscious (Peer, 2019).

Meditation and therapy also enable people to gain a deeper understanding of themselves and thereby become more conscious and present in their day-to-day lives. I am not saying you need therapy, though I do believe that talking about our feelings and experiences with someone with a neutral viewpoint is highly beneficial. We all want to feel loved, accepted, and free, but in order to experience the true nature of those feelings, it is necessary to know yourself first.

Tapping Into the Subconscious, Kavi's Story

Kavi, a 17-year-old girl in the 11th grade, was a bright student who often found herself struggling with impulsive reactions and strong emotions that she couldn't control or understand. Kavi had struggled with this for as long as she could remember. After shouting at her favorite teacher for an assignment she felt was pointless, Kavi was determined to get to the bottom of her impulses. Her friends told her they agreed with her about the assignment but that yelling doesn't get you anything but trouble. For some reason, though Kavi knew this, she couldn't help but burst when she felt strongly about something.

That day, Kavi was told to stay after class to speak with the teacher about her behavior. This was nothing new for Kavi, but this time, she decided to advocate for herself.

"Ms. Raju, sometimes I can't help but shout when I feel something strongly. It's like a volcano that has to erupt, or it'll spread through my body and melt me from the inside out," Kavi explained. "I don't like the assignment, but I know that my reaction was inappropriate. If you're not too angry, do you think you could help me?"

Ms. Raju sighed and smiled. "Kavi," she said, "I'm proud of you for recognizing that. It is difficult to feel so strongly, and learning how to release that energy takes time. I will make an appointment with our school counselor for you. I bet she can give you some helpful tips."

"Thanks. I'll check in with Ms. Simpson tomorrow."

Ms. Raju made an appointment, and the next day, Kavi walked into Ms. Simpson's office with determination.

"Okay, Ms. Simpson, do your thing. Fix me," Kavi told her.

"Hi there, Kavi. Why don't you have a seat? There's no fixing to be done," the counselor said, "Oftentimes, the root of our problems can be found in the subconscious—the part of your mind that stores all of your experiences."

Kavi listened to Ms. Simpson explain how the subconscious mind is often responsible for and an influencer of our behavior, reactions, and emotions. Much like a computer, the mind can be programmed too. Our experiences, beliefs, and habits program our levels of consciousness and have a huge impact on our lives. Kavi also learned that the brain reacts differently depending on external factors. For example, we may be quick to anger if we are hungry, didn't get enough sleep, or had an argument with a parent, friend, or partner. Perhaps you have a parent who always says "no" and shows no interest in your interests. In that case, a teacher assigning something you don't care about could be a trigger. This means that an experience held in our subconscious is provoked and causes a reaction that doesn't fit the present scenario.

Kavi didn't want to see Ms. Simpson every week because it cut into the time she had with her friends, so instead, Ms. Simpson began giving Kavi some homework. She'd offer links to websites with meditations or offer journal prompts and visualization techniques to tap into her subconscious mind to help Kavi learn where her big feelings originated. Over time, Kavi's knowledge of herself increased and allowed her to gain more control over her reactions. She became more self-aware and understood the link between her behavior and her subconscious mind.

Though Kavi still had emotional outbursts, she was better able to control her emotions and tried to control her reactions. She learned that it wasn't the anger getting her into trouble but the reaction to the situation that caused the anger. This allowed her to choose a reaction that would work in her favor rather than against her.

Mindful Meditation

Nothing ever goes away until it has taught us what we need to know.

–Pema Chodron

Have you ever tried to forget something that embarrassed you or something that had happened in your life, but your mind just wouldn't let it go? Some people believe that every experience is an opportunity to learn more about yourself, and until you figure out the lesson, you may not be able to shake that particular feeling, memory, or idea. The subconscious holds onto the event and the conscious mind won't let you forget. While a loving-kindness meditation can cultivate feelings of compassion for loved ones and enemies, I recommend that for this portion of the book, you do the following meditation for yourself. Do it for the little girl in you who is begging to be loved, accepted and freed.

Meditation is the practice of tapping into the mind and cultivating awareness of self. Only when we know ourselves can we make the choice to live freely. Learning how to mindfully notice our thoughts enables us to react more compassionately and allows us to change the way we speak to ourselves and others. Below is a practice to help cultivate love and kindness for yourself. Acknowledge that your problems are not unique to you and that somewhere in the world, others experience similar feelings. You are not alone. Learning to love yourself will liberate you from so many constraints (Mindworks Team, 2019).

I recommend having a journal close by to record any thoughts before and after the practice. It also may be nice to set a chime on your phone and a timer to begin and end the meditation. I'd say five minutes is a good start. Follow these steps from Mindworks Meditation (Mindworks Team, 2019):

Find a comfortable seated position either on a chair or on a cushion on the floor. Preferably in a quiet space where you are not likely to be interrupted.

Sit upright with a straight spine.

Roll your shoulders up toward your ears and down your back.

Breathe.

Fix your gaze somewhere in front of you.

Notice the rise and fall of your chest or belly as you inhale through the nose and exhale through the mouth.

Put one hand over your belly and the other over your heart.

Breathe.

Inhale fully.

Exhale completely.

Notice the connection between your body and the chair, floor, or cushion.

Feel the weight of your body sink into the seat.

Breathe.

Any thoughts that come up, try not to dwell on one in particular. Simply notice the thought, inhale to acknowledge it, exhale to release it. Breathe.

Try to observe your thoughts rather than control or judge them.

Bring your attention to the breath.

Notice the depth of your inhale.

Follow the entire exhale and notice the moment of pause before the next inhale.

Breathe.

Bring your attention to the sensation of the hands on the body.

Notice the temperature.

Notice any emotions brought on by holding yourself in this way.

Breathe.

Follow the breath for the next three inhales and exhales.

On the last exhale, hold for one, two, three.

Exhale through the mouth, sighing.

On the following inhale, bring to mind the image of yourself as a young child.

Notice any emotions that arise or any resistance to this image.

Watch your thoughts pass by as clouds floating across the sky.

Holding on to this image of yourself as a child, speak to her softly repeating these words:

May you be happy.

May you be safe.

May you be healthy.

May you experience joy and love.

May you live with peace and ease.

Breathe.

Keeping your hands on your body, take the deepest inhale through the nose.

Sigh and exhale through the mouth. Repeat three times. Deep inhale. Full exhale.

Return to your normal rhythm of breath.

Bring to mind your self-image as you are right now.

Imagine the room you are in and the position of your body.

Imagine you are sitting across from yourself and just breathe. Breathe in your own company.

Inhale fully.

Exhale completely.

On each inhale and exhale, repeat the following words for yourself:

I am happy.

I am safe.

I am healthy.

I experience joy and love.

I live with peace and ease.

Breathe.

Allow the images of yourself and your inner child fade away and just be you. In this moment. In this room.

Follow your breath for the remainder of this practice and notice how you feel in the moments before going back to your day.

Chapter 2: Challenging Self Beliefs

I don't think that loving yourself is a choice. I think that it's a decision that has to be made for survival. –Lizzo

Self-beliefs have the power to carry us forward to live a life in which we thrive, and they have the power to hold us back from achieving or even realizing our dreams. How you see yourself, speak to yourself, and speak about yourself impacts how you interact with the world and others. It influences the kind of choices you will make, the opportunities you will take or miss, the quality of the relationships you build, and so much more. Lizzo is right in saying that loving yourself is a decision you must make to survive in this world, because so many things, from social media to friends and from family to school to government systems, will try to tear you down, break you, and convince you that you must fit into their mold. No matter how shattered you may feel, you always have the choice to come into the light. Anyone can learn to love themselves, and in order to do so, one must remain open to change, learning, and challenging personal beliefs and be dedicated to discovering and embracing your true self (Lyness, 2018).

Other People

I know for sure what we dwell on is who we become.

–Oprah Winfrey

Below, you will find three stories of teen girls navigating middle and high school. Notice any emotions evoked by reading their experiences. Pay attention to the one that stands out the most to you and ask yourself why this may be.

Aaliyah

Aaliyah is in the 10th grade. She studies and pays attention in class (most of the time), tries her best, and asks questions when she doesn't understand. Aaliyah doesn't get amazing grades, but they aren't terrible either, and she's usually proud of her efforts. She loves to play basketball after school with her friends, but on the team, she only gets to play if someone else is injured; still, she is at every practice and game giving it her all.

Aaliyah has a phone to communicate with her friends and family, but her parents don't allow her to use it 24-7, and they frequently remind her that filters are not real life, that true beauty is in her soul not her clothing. She likes to hike outside and go to the beach. She watches movies, plays Nintendo, draws, and builds masterpieces with LEGOs. When Aaliyah answers a question wrong in class, she sometimes feels a bit embarrassed, but she'll answer another. If she trips on the basketball court, she gets back up and keeps playing. When a kid at school calls her names, though it does hurt her feelings, she always responds in the same way: "I know who I am. It's okay if you don't."

When Aaliyah sees her friends or peers succeed, she cheers them on and celebrates them. When she succeeds, she celebrates herself as well, and when she fails, she notices what went wrong and tries not to repeat the same mistakes. While Aaliyah is like any other human who sometimes worries about their looks or how others perceive them, she is different in the fact that she knows her worth. She doesn't compare herself to others; she sees their good qualities just as she sees her own. If someone makes Aaliyah feel unimportant or uncared for, she either decreases the time she spends around this person, or she confronts the person to try to solve the problem. She is conscious of her feelings as well as the experiences and people that bring out positive or negative reactions in her. This knowledge makes it easier for her to surround herself with people who lift her up rather than hold her down.

Alliyah knows deep inside that her worth is not diminished by anything. She knows she is worthy of love and respect and kindness and opportunity. She believes she is capable, even when sometimes she isn't. Because of this, Aaliyah lives a happy life. She has ups and downs, but overall, she is content being herself and those she invites into her life love her for who she is.

How you love yourself is how you teach others to love you.

–Rupi Kaur

Dani

Dani is in the 12th grade. She rarely engages in class and avoids answering questions even when she knows the answer. She can pass without studying and does the bare minimum on assignments, anything to go unnoticed. She's an insanely talented dancer but refuses to do so outside of her bedroom. One time, the school's dance team coach caught her dancing alone in the gym and raved about how amazing she was and how she had to join the team. Dani turned down the offer, not wanting anyone to see her dance. That year, the team got to travel out of the country for a competition.

Dani loves to write but never lets anyone read her ideas. Her English teacher invited her to a writer's conference where there would be teenage writers from all over the region as well as well-known authors giving small workshops. Dani declined the invite because she worried she wouldn't be as good as the other kids there.

Her parents gave her a phone when she was 13 with no rules or regulations to its use. They didn't talk to her about what she might see or monitor the length of time she spends scrolling through social media. Dani often compares herself to what she sees online, usually looking for flaws in herself.

Dani believes that she is mediocre at best. She doesn't think she's smart enough, attractive enough, brave enough, or worthy enough to take chances or succeed. Dani never accepts a compliment and doesn't think anyone really likes her. She compares herself to others, and when they succeed, she doesn't celebrate them. She criticizes herself instead. Dani misses a lot of wonderful opportunities because she worries about what other people think of her more than what she thinks of herself.

When you stop living your life based on what others think of you, real life begins. At that moment, you will finally see the door to self-acceptance opened. –Shannon L. Alder

Xin

Xin is in the 8th grade. She is shy and doesn't often like to be the center of attention. Her drama class was putting on a play for the younger grades, and her teacher asked her to take one of the acting roles. Xin hesitated and hoped to work with the sound crew instead, but her classmates told her she should try the role because it was perfect for her. Though she was nervous, after listening to her teacher and classmates encourage her to take a risk, she chose to do it.

Xin spent every day at lunch rehearsing with the rest of the cast, and the night before the performance, she couldn't sleep. Xin tossed and turned in her bed for hours and when she finally fell asleep, she dreamed of getting on stage and forgetting her lines. As soon as the sun rose, Xin texted her friend who was also in the play to tell her she was sick and couldn't perform. To her surprise, her friend was also a ball of nerves and had a similar night to Xin's. They agreed to go to school together and practice during their morning break. Her friend reminded her that they had made a commitment and the rest of the cast was depending on them regardless of their fears.

"But I'm so scared," Xin said. "What if I forget my lines?"

"We're performing for the fifth graders, Xin. Even if you do forget your lines, they don't know what you're supposed to say, so just go with it. Do it scared. It'll be over by this afternoon and then we get to have a pizza party with the cast."

Xin took a deep breath and continued to rehearse with her friend. During the performance, Xin remembered most of her lines, and the ones she forgot, the rest of the cast filled in without anyone in the audience noticing. After the show, everyone's energy was high. Xin couldn't stop apologizing for messing up a few lines. Eventually, her friend put her hands on her face, looked directly into her eyes, and told her, "You did it, Xin! Listen!"

The cast quieted down and heard the cheers of the audience. They walked back on the stage, and the teacher introduced the cast members one by one for extra applause. Xin beamed on stage, and when it was over, her teacher asked her to join the drama club.

"But I forgot my lines and I was so nervous," Xin said.

"Did you have fun? Did you remember most of your lines? Did the cast help you out? Did the audience cheer?" her teacher asked, knowing the answer to all questions was "yes."

"Okay," Xin agreed. "I'll try."

The following day, Xin went into the drama club, and though she was shy in her life, on stage, she learned to come out of her shell a bit and discovered a new passion that she would pursue for the rest of her school career.

Stay afraid but do it anyway. What's important is the action. You don't have to wait to be confident. Just do it and eventually the confidence will follow. –Carrie Fisher

Journal Prompts

If you don't see a clear path for what you want, sometimes you have to make it yourself. –Mindy Kaling.

Some people call it keeping a diary; others call it journaling. Either way, the act of writing down your thoughts, feelings, and ideas can help you experience them with self-compassion. It is a form of release to speak or write your thoughts, getting them out of your body and into the open. Oftentimes, people hold themselves back, not really saying what they think out of worry of being wrong or offending someone, but a journal provides a nonjudgmental space free from the fear of punishment where you can voice your struggles and fears, emotions, and experiences (Andy Milne, 2019).

Writing helps build emotional intelligence and enables you to be more mindful and aware of your thoughts as you will begin to take notice of patterns you might not have otherwise noticed. You may build self-confidence as you write and reflect on what you have written, and you may take notice of what makes you feel upset or angry, how you react to unexpected situations, and when you feel free and happy. This self-awareness will naturally transfer into your thought patterns, and slowly but surely, you will be able to release any self-doubt that you carry (Andy Milne, 2019).

I encourage you to start keeping a journal if you don't already. I prefer to free write with a pen or pencil, which means to just write whatever comes into my mind without caring if I'm on the lines, spelling correctly, or even writing legibly. It is the act of writing my stream of consciousness that is helpful. However, if this is not your preference, begin by writing about your day, your struggles, your moments of joy, etc. Below are some suggestions that can get you started. You can record your thoughts here or in a personal journal later.

1. Which of the above people do you think reflects you? What about their story resonates with you?

_____

_____

_____

_____

2. Notice some of the personal qualities of each person. Which ones come to mind first? Were they negative or positive?

_____

_____

_____

_____

_____

_____

_____

_____

_____

_____

_____

_____

_____

_____

3. Choose your favorite quote within this chapter and write it somewhere you will read it every day. Notice how this makes you feel each time you read it.

_____

_____

_____

_____

_____

_____

_____

_____

4. When do you feel good about yourself?

_____

_____

_____

_____

_____

_____

_____

_____

_____

5. Write a list of 10 things you are proud of.

_____

_____

_____

_____

_____

_____

_____

_____

_____

_____

_____

_____

_____

_____

_____

_____

_____

_____

_____

Chapter 3: Attitude Matters

I am learning every day to allow the space between where I am and where I want to be to inspire me and not terrify me.

–Tracee Ellis Ross

The truth is, more than 85% of people suffer from self-doubt. This goes to show that the ebb and flow of emotions is innately human and that most people doubt themselves, some more often than others. Do not pass judgment on yourself for the way you think; pay attention to your inner voice and take an interest in increasing your optimistic outlook. It is a choice to train your brain to focus more on possibility than on failure. It might be something that becomes routine and natural for you, it might be something you will have to work on every day, and it is worth working on (Morales, 2021).

We are all going through this thing we call life doing the best we can. Experiencing feelings and creating relationships. You only live this life once. If you wouldn't say it to your best friend, you probably shouldn't say it to yourself either. Be kind.

Choosing to be inspired instead of terrified is not a simple thing to do for everyone, especially if you struggle with low self-esteem, anxiety, or depression. The choice is not as easy as just saying, "I'll be happy today." Our emotions don't work that way, but our attitudes can be changed overtime with dedication to the process. An inspired mindset can help you navigate difficult situations and challenges more easily than a scared mindset (Morales, 2021).

When faced with a difficult task or even a new opportunity, some people feel overwhelmed and scared, while others feel energized and excited. Shifting perspective is to focus on possibilities rather than challenges or failures. When faced with a challenge, instead of focusing only on the potential problems, try to find a positive that could come from the situation. If you can't find one, remind yourself that it will not last forever, that you will get through whatever it is, and that all you can do is try your best and that your best will be different on different days (Morales, 2021).

Attitude can have a significant impact not only on the life of a teen but on anyone's life. A positive attitude can lead to better mental and physical health, stronger relationships, and more success in school and extracurricular activities. On the other hand, a negative attitude can lead to increased stress, poor self-esteem, and difficulty achieving goals. A positive attitude can make it easier to handle difficult situations and challenges, while a negative attitude can make them feel overwhelming. When we let our emotions take over our logic, we often make mistakes, say things we later regret, or allow them to create mental blocks that can feel impossible to break down. It is a learned skill to process information and react appropriately; no one is born with this. A toddler doesn't wait for Mama to finish making dinner before crying and begging for playtime. We are taught to be patient, ask politely, and behave respectfully. It is equally as important to learn self-love and appreciation, for without that, our attitudes would never change (Cherry, 2021).

Developing a positive attitude will help you to move through life with the ability to see the bright side, to overcome challenges rather than shy away from or be defeated by them. Learning how to manage the wide range of human emotions is vital to living a balanced, open-minded, happy life. Our attitudes are influenced by many factors including our upbringing and life experiences, and while these are sometimes deeply embedded, they are possible to change (Cherry, 2021).

I will emphasize that there are situations that are too overwhelming to bear, and shifting your mindset may be difficult. In these moments, listen to your body and rest or move if you need to, take time to write about it, talk to someone you trust, ask for help, or go outside. Practice self-care by allowing yourself to feel whatever you feel without holding back.

Reframing the Mind

Every morning is a fresh start. Wake up with a thankful heart.

–Kristen Butler

The kind of life we are raised in is out of our control, and we have little choice in the matter until we are adults and can make decisions to build the kind of life we want. While having a rough life is not a choice, choosing a positive attitude can help you navigate the challenges you face and find happiness amid the difficult situations. Regardless of your upbringing, having a positive attitude is a powerful tool in coping with difficult circumstances as it inspires you to find ways to improve your situation while a negative attitude finds ways to keep you down (Cullins, 2017).

This is not to be confused with the people who are always saying, "Being happy all the time is a choice," "Other people have it worse," "You should find the silver lining," or "Let it go; it's been long enough." Having a positive attitude does not mean that feeling anger, sadness, frustration, or irritation are bad emotions or even emotions that you need to get over, stop, push through, or forget. There's no such thing as bad emotions, just emotions; all humans have them and some animals too. Feelings are how humans process information. If your grandmother dies, people don't say, "That's life. Everyone dies." They tell you to rest and to reach out if you need anything. They bring you food, call you to check in, and ask how you're feeling. That is because you need to go through your feelings to continue living your life. We are encouraged to accept and process our emotions in life altering-situations, and we should give ourselves the same level of compassion as we grow and learn and develop our mind (Cullins, 2017).

Tips for Developing a Positive Attitude

In the current world, everyone is exposed to horrifying news from around the world on a daily basis. Whether in the midst of crisis or reading about it, having a positive mindset does not come easily, especially to those living in conflict. Even the most optimistic of people are not immune to the impact of the constant influx of negative information. The remainder of this chapter provides an abundance of steps you can take to increase the joy and positivity in your life which can help you to navigate challenging situations and feelings.

Be sure not to overwhelm yourself further by thinking you must do all of these things right now. Any habit takes time to build and this is no exception. I would suggest, after reading through the chapter of tips for developing a positive attitude, to notice if you do any of them already, then choose one to add or begin with. I like to set reminders on my phone. For example, an app called Presently sends me one notification per day to remind me to record something I'm grateful for in that moment. Little steps amount to so much more than we sometimes think, and in the case of building positivity, every little bit counts and is worth celebrating.

Set Realistic Goals and Work Toward Achieving Them
(Cullins, 2017)

Sarah is a 16-year-old girl with a lot of personal goals, but she often struggles to achieve them. The day she returned to school after winter break, her teacher had the class make a list of goals they wanted to achieve before the end of the school year. Excited about the task, Sarah proceeded to write a long list of goals and was eager to share them with the class.

"I will get above 95% on every test and assignment. I will have enough money by the summer to take a road trip with my friend. I will convince my mom to let us do this local trip. I will be the best artist in class, and I will be captain of the track and field team. I will read at least 50 books, and I will write my own novel," Sarah listed almost all in one breath.

The class was silent for a moment until…

"Umm, those are great goals, Sarah, but how can one person achieve all of that in just six months?" a classmate asked.

"Yeah, that's not possible. Besides, why do you always have to be the best at everything?" a classmate asked.

"I think Sarah can do anything she wants," her friend defended.

Sarah felt her cheeks blush, she immediately sat down and hoped her teacher would call on someone else so she could sink into her chair.

"Having goals and writing them down is only the first step. It is easy to write lists of what we hope to achieve, but the important part of achieving big goals is to set small ones that bring us closer to the big ones," Sarah's teacher explained. "For example, Sarah, if you want to save money, how are you going to do that? Do you have a job or get an allowance?"

Sarah shook her head no.

"Okay, so the big goal is to save money?"

Sarah nodded yes.

"So, in order to do that, you must first set goals to get there. For example, make a resume and get a job, then decide how much you will save each time you get paid between now and June in order to go on your trip."

Sarah smiled and wrote what her teacher had said.

"I challenge the entire class to create two big goals to achieve by the end of June," the teacher said. "Each of your big goals needs to be broken down into steps to help you achieve them. You are required to reflect on your progress at least once a week."

Sarah decided that her two big goals would be to save money and to get high grades. She knew that in order to do this, she would need to find a job first. To get good grades, she would need to study, and in order to work toward both goals, she would have to learn time management.

"That's only three things," Sarah thought. "I can do that."

Sarah wrote her big goals on paper and posted them to the bulletin board above her desk at home. Beneath those, she wrote out the steps to achieving the goals in checklist format and each time she achieved a goal, she put a checkmark in the box. Each day, she saw the chart in her room, and this kept the positive goals in her consciousness, enabling her to keep a more positive attitude because she could see her achievements along the way.

Example:

Save Money

     Learn how to make resume

     Print and distribute resumes to local places

     Practice interviewing with YI

     Get a job

     Ask for help to open a savings account

Get Above 95% on all School work

     Make a study schedule

     Keep a visible calendar for upcoming due dates

Find a study partner

Convince Mom of Road Trip with Yi

Share photos of Polly's Cove with mom

Show her I am responsible

Know my schedule without having to be reminded

It took some time, but Sarah stuck to her goals, and by June, she'd achieved all but one- her mom wouldn't let her go on a road trip by herself with Yi. But she did let her drive all the way to Polly's Cove with Yi sitting in the passenger's seat and her mom sitting in the back, holding on to the safety handle the entire three-hour drive.

* * *

I challenge you to come up with one to three big goals and break them down into smaller, achievable goals like Sarah did and notice how your outlook changes. Below is some space for you or you may choose to do this in a personal journal. Do not feel any pressure to fill in all the lines or to work toward more than one goal at a time. The smaller, more achievable goals will enable you to build a positive mindset and make it more likely that you will achieve your bigger goals. Life isn't always easy, and a lot of the time, it's confusing and stirs up all the feelings. Setting goals creates a positive focus for your mind amid the chaos.

Big Goal

        Step 1 _____

        Step 2 _____

        Step 3 _____

Big Goal

        Step 1 _____

        Step 2 _____

        Step 3 _____

Big Goal

        Step 1 _____

        Step 2 _____

        Step 3 _____

Record Moments of Happiness and Gratitude and Share with Others (Cullins, 2017)

Jai was having a normal day. She was home on a Sunday afternoon, doing nothing besides lounging around the house.

Her parents were gardening, her brother was at choir practice, and Jai was about to crawl back into bed with a book when she got a text from her friend.

Vi: COME OVER RIGHT NOW!

Jai: Why? Just tell me here.

Vi: No. This is too big not to see your face when I tell you. You're never gonna believe it!

Jai: Did Dylan finally ask you out? lol

Vi: Pssh, no. Better than that.

Jai: Jayden?

Vi: NO! It's not about a boy, just get dressed and come over!

Jai: . . . . TELL ME!

Vi: Hurry up or I'm posting it online before I tell you.

Jai: Coming!

Jai had no idea what Vi could be talking about. All she's talked about for weeks were Dylan and Jayden. Jai quickly threw on some clothes, threw her hair up in a messy bun, and ran out the door on the way down the block to Vi's house.

"JAI!" Vi hollered down the street, jumping with tears streaming down her face. "Jai!"

As soon as Jai heard her name, she ran as fast as she could. Her heart was racing, and her mind was jumping from one possibility to the other. Her lazy feelings were now replaced with excitement and wonder.

"Jai! I got in, I got in!" Vi cried and laughed and hugged Jai as soon as she was close enough. "I did it, Jai! I got in!"

Sharing in Vi's energy, Jai was jumping with her friend and congratulating her and crying out of joy herself until she realized she still had no idea what Vi was talking about.

"Got in where?" she asked.

"The Youth Symphony!! I got in!" Vi cried.

"AHHHHHHH!" Jai screamed in shared excitement. She had forgotten about Vi's auditions that took place months prior to receiving the news.

The two friends celebrated the achievement for the rest of the day.

* * *

Before continuing, I encourage you to answer the questions and to continue this practice in your own journal. You will always have something to remind yourself of the moments where you felt uplifted.

Moments of gratitude:

_____

_____

_____

_____

_____

_____

_____

Emotions I feel:

_____

_____

_____

_____

_____

_____

_____

Who I shared with:

_____

_____

_____

_____

_____

Surround Yourself with Positive People (Cullins, 2017)

Imitating those around us is called *limbic synchrony*. Imitation is present before we are even born as it is proven that babies' heartbeats take on the same rhythm as their mothers. Nerve cells in the brain referred to as *mirror neurons* are responsible for imitating behaviors. For example, research shows that if a person hears laughter, the brain sends signals to prepare the muscles in the face for laughter. Other examples of mirroring include yawning when someone else yawns, crossing your legs or arms if the person you're with does so, asking what your date is going to order before making your decision, and displaying sadness at a funeral even if you didn't have a personal relationship with the person. There are many forms of nonverbal communication that human beings use to show trust, empathy, and understanding. If we can make ourselves aware of this fact and of whom we imitate, we can distinguish between who brings a positive light into our lives and who darkens the room, so-to-speak (Johnston & Kelly, 2017).

It is a fact that relationships change over time because people change over time. It is natural to outgrow friendships and to set boundaries for your personal happiness. While losing a friend or ending a relationship is heartbreaking, choosing to surround yourself with people who love you, celebrate you, and lift your attitude is always going to be better than holding onto a relationship that makes you doubt yourself or leaves you feeling drained.

In the above story, Vi shared her happiness with Jai, which lifted both of their attitudes. This happens when we share in each other's emotions. If you were in a room full of people crying, you would likely become sad as well, mirroring those around you; similarly, if you are surrounded by people laughing, you are likely to join in the laughter too. Develop your positive attitude by recording and sharing moments of happiness as well as embracing the joy of others (Johnston & Kelly, 2017).

Some people come into our lives and quickly go. Some people stay for a while and move our souls to dance. They awaken us to a new understanding, leave footprints on our hearts, and we are never, ever the same. –Flavia Weedn

* * * *

In the space below or in a personal journal, make a list of the people you spend most of your time with and begin to record how you feel before, during, and after interacting with them. What do you notice now that you did not notice before? Are there any actions you can take to increase the positive feelings and decrease the more difficult feelings?

Person _____

How do I feel before seeing this person?

_____

How do I feel when I am with this person?

_____

How do I feel after spending time with this person?

_____

Person _____

How do I feel before seeing this person?

_____

How do I feel when I am with this person?

_____

How do I feel after spending time with this person?

_____

Person _____

How do I feel before seeing this person?

_____

How do I feel when I am with this person?

_____

How do I feel after spending time with this person?

_____

Engage in Activities You Enjoy (Cullins, 2017)

Figure out what you like to do and do more of that. Oftentimes, as teenagers, you are told what to do, what to wear, and where to be and when. You live at the mercy of others dictating what you eat and where you go. Finding activities and hobbies that you enjoy doing gives you the opportunity to cultivate joy within yourself regardless of what goes on around you. If you don't know what you like to do, try a bunch of different things until you find something that gets you excited. If money is of concern, many places make it possible to receive government assistance to join sports or participate in the arts, and plenty of activities are free (S.R, 2022).

Hobbies give you something to look forward to and boost your mental health. Hobbies can be exciting, like a new sport, singing, dancing, or acting, or hobbies can be quieter, like meditation, yoga, hiking, and reading. Whatever you choose, try to make time for it as often as you can. Studies show that partaking in things that boost your joy can increase overall happiness as the feelings cultivated during the activity can remain in the body for days. When choosing your hobbies, be sure not to choose things you think you should do just because your friends or siblings do them or things that will cause more stress and frustration than joy. Take time and learn more about yourself by trying new things (S.R, 2022).

* * * *

In your journal, I encourage you to draw a big sun with a circle in the middle and triangle rays all around. Write all of your current interests and hobbies in the circle. On each sun ray, write something new that you'd like to try.

Spend Time Outside and in Nature

In a world of constant change and streaming technology, I find solace in the forest where a tree remains a tree.

–Angie Weiland-Crosby

Spending time in nature is proven to reduce feelings of anger and stress, invite mindfulness, help you to be active, and provide opportunities for meeting new people. It is also a place to be the most yourself. You can immerse in nature and spend time with yourself, listening to the sounds of the earth bringing a sense of calm throughout your body. It can reduce the feeling of loneliness, and overall helps you feel more relaxed (Cullins, 2017; Mind, 2021).

Training the mind to be fully in the moment is a lifelong practice not an end goal. It is human nature to think; the goal is not to stop our thoughts but to take our focus from them and turn it toward nature, toward the breeze, the trees, the sand, and the sea. We all have a thought process and are constantly stimulated by our surroundings. Retreating into nature removes distraction and enables you to be here now. Some people feel the most connected to nature when hiking mountains or walking through the forest or jungle. Others gain feelings of calm and comfort from being by the sea or near large bodies of water. Still more enjoy a stroll through a park or on a trail by a river, or simply sitting in a natural environment away from buildings or manmade noise. No matter your choice of nature to connect to, I am certain you will find your space, source of calm, and safety. For me, it's the ocean. For a dear friend, it's the mountains. For my son, it's the woods. Find your calm and spend time there whenever you get the chance.

I recommend that time spent in nature be device-free, but I'm as guilty as the next person for wanting beautiful photos of nature, so if you must bring your phone, turn it to silent to avoid interrupting nature's peace, and go long periods of time without touching it.

* * * *

In your own journal, make a list or draw different shapes to fill in with outdoor spaces and activities you enjoy and new ones in which you'd like to explore. Note which emotions are present for you in each of the natural spaces and activities. Is it a higher energy with a happy, exciting feeling or a lower energy with calm, serene, peaceful feelings? Are there ways you can incorporate more time for these activities and spaces into your life?

Practice Mindfulness by Focusing on the Present Moment

I'm supposed to be unhappy without someone, but aren't I someone? –
Billie Eilish

You are someone! You are the most important person in your life, and it is yourself with whom you spend the most time. Rather than searching for validation from others, appreciate yourself and find enjoyment in being in your own company. Bringing your mind to the present moment, not ignoring worries about the past or desires for the future, and instead allowing them to pass by and being here now is a powerful skill. This can enable you to navigate life with an attitude that will help you thrive and shine as opposed to one that is always searching for meaning from other people (Cullins, 2017).

Activities that can help you become present could be meditation and following your breath, stretching and connecting your breath to each movement, blowing bubbles, watching ants climb up and down the trunk of a tree, watching a leaf blow in the wind, listening to the repetitive crash of waves, or doing anything that focuses the mind on what is happening right now that can bring a sense of peace and calm over the body, enabling you to refocus the mind and gain control over your reactions.

Practicing mindfulness is simply just paying attention to what is happening in the present moment via your five senses. It is not about achieving a goal or clearing your mind, it is about having an honest look at what you are experiencing right now. This practice can decrease stress levels and has proven to show higher academic performance along with increased self-control and focus (Willard, 2020).

* * * *

Read the exercises below and try one, remembering they are always here for you to come back to.

- Follow your breath.

- Stand barefoot outside.

- Color.

- Notice your surroundings.

- Go for a walk outside.

- Do a puzzle.

- Tune in to your senses: What do you see, smell, touch, taste, hear, and feel?

- Place one hand on your belly and the other over your heart. Hold. Breathe.

- Paint.

- Write in a journal.

- Cuddle a pet or stuffy.

Help Others

Hope is not something that you have. Hope is something that you create, with your actions. Hope is contagious. Other people start acting in a way that has more hope. –Alexandria Ocasio-Cortez

Helping other people is proven to boost self-confidence and cultivate a positive attitude and feelings of joy and hope. While teens are often encouraged to volunteer, the emphasis is often placed on what it does for you, like boosting your resume or your college application. Maybe your crush volunteers, so you join to spend more time with them. Perhaps you volunteer because you like being able to tell others that you are so selfless. These reasons are not the ones I am talking about. To freely give your time without expecting anything in return is a way to show love and care to others who may not have otherwise felt those emotions. To like others is to like yourself. We should be encouraged to help others not because we want something but because showing compassion is a vital aspect of being human and creating a safe and loving community (Cullins, 2017).

As we learned about mirroring through the section about surrounding yourself with positive people, volunteering is an act of love, an act of kindness. Those are the kinds of behaviors we want people to mirror. Those acts are ones that change the world.

* * * *

In your journal, record the suggestions below and add to the list or draw different shapes to fill in with the ways in which you already help others.

- Coach an elementary sports team.

- Volunteer to run a club at school or at a local elementary school.

- Read to senior adults or elementary students.

- Volunteer locally. (Ask your family or teachers about where to start.)

- Support a cause you are passionate about.

- Pick up trash in your neighborhood.

Chapter 4: Perspective

I could walk a mile in your shoes, but I already know they're just as uncomfortable as mine. Let's walk next to each other instead...

–Lynda Meyers

I imagine you've often been asked to see things from other points of view. Perhaps as a child, you read the book, *Duck! Rabbit!* written by Amy Krouse Rosenthal and illustrated by Tom Lichtenheld, in which the narrators argue over if the drawing in the book is in fact a duck or a rabbit. Or maybe you've seen the meme with the two people standing on either end of a number debating whether it's a 6 or a 9. Another popular kid's book you may have read, *Seven Blind Mice* written by Ed Young, in which each of the mice is blind and feels a different part of an elephant, speculating as to what it actually is. All of these things aim to teach you that it is important to get the whole picture, to look at things from all sides before forming your opinion or at least to remain open-minded and willing to change your opinion when you gain new information.

Seeing things from another point of view is a learned skill that takes practice and a present mind. Now that you're older, these stories and images might prove to be easy for you to see all options. Perhaps you've witnessed more complete imagery and been able to find a multitude of things you didn't see at first glance. For young children, the concept of perspective is more easily grasped through pictures and modeling, whereas older kids, teens, and even adults need a bit more. Sure, we can find things in photos, but in life, changing our perspective about a situation, experience, or understanding is much more difficult than just turning the page.

The more we increase our awareness of the present moment, the more clearly we see and understand. In moments of heightened emotion, you must make a conscious effort to choose your words and response to the situation rather than immediately reacting (which is what most people do). Remind yourself that we are all living in our heads, that we all bring personal experiences to any given situation, that there is no way that we can know every detail of someone else's life, and as such, we should not assume intent without clarification. Walk together, knowing that though you are currently in disagreement, you both carry your own stories and are capable of offering empathy for one another (Abernethy, 2020).

This doesn't only apply to arguments or disagreements with others, but to personal dilemmas and challenges as well. Gaining perspective can provide you with tools to help you move through self-doubt rather than drowning in it. As the brain's job is to protect you at all costs, jumping to conclusions, acting out, and not fully processing situations based on the brain's immediate interpretations of a moment, the body often reacts first rather than responds. To react is to act impulsively based only on your immediate emotional state. To respond is to thoughtfully consider the situation as a whole and choose your response in a way that supports your beliefs (Abernethy, 2020).

Things Are Not Always as They Seem

The most common way people give up their power is by believing they don't have any. –Alice Walker

The brain is a complex organ that is the control center of our very being, responsible for making sense of the world, all while making us the star, the most important being on the planet. Perspective taking is the ability to change our brain's natural course and remove ourselves from the center in order to gain understanding from other points of view (Abernethy, 2020).

Perspective taking is also the ability to question your thoughts about a situation. For example, when working toward a goal, whether mental, like training the brain to focus on possibility rather than failure, emotional, like being able to identify your feelings and things that bring them up, or physical, like running a marathon or increasing flexibility and strength, oftentimes the hardest parts are getting started and sticking with it (Abernethy, 2020).

In a world where we have everything at our fingertips, human beings have evolved to beings in need of instant gratification. Long-term goals often take time, energy, patience, dedication to the process, and numerous battles with self-doubt creeping in to tell you this is too hard, it's not working, or you cannot do this. Continue to the stories below for perspective, inspiration, and reflection.

Long-Distance Swimmer, Florence Chadwick

You may not have heard of Florence Chadwick as her first big swim happened in 1952, long before your time, but her story is one that evokes reflection and thought. She is a woman who swam from England to France and from France to England who was also the first woman to ever attempt and successfully swim between the California coastline and Catalina Island (Maccarone, 2018). Try to put yourself in her position for a moment.

Imagine you are the first woman to attempt this strenuous swim, and you have a team following alongside in a boat. This might not sound so bad if you're deep into the school year and just wish to relax on a beach, but this is not a leisurely day at the beach. This strenuous swim is 26 miles long and will take a minimum of 16 hours for an experienced swimmer to complete (Maccarone, 2018).

Imagine diving into the water by yourself knowing that the team following you is there to watch out for sharks who inevitably swarm you, to be ready in case of unexpected injury, fatigue, or cramps, and to offer food along the way. As you get deeper into the swim, the waters are so rough that you need to take seasickness medication, but you don't give up. You believe you can do this, and you keep going. Your mom is there with you too, cheering you on and supporting you every stroke of the way (Maccarone, 2018).

Unfortunately, as you approach hour 15 of the swim, a thick fog surrounds you just moments after hearing your safety crew use rifles to scare away the prowling sharks. You can no longer see more than a few inches in any direction, the boat is in the mist, and you are beyond exhausted. All of this begins to eat away at your mind. You feel frightened, you start questioning whether or not you can do this, whether or not you are strong enough to finish the swim. It is less than an hour before the unknown and self-doubt take over your previous ambition, and you decide to end the journey by requesting to get into the boat (Maccarone, 2018).

Cold, tired, and disappointed, you learn rather quickly that if only you had continued on for one more mile, you would have reached the beaches of Catalina Island (Maccarone, 2018). Imagine that feeling. All of your training, hard work, and determination brought down by some fog and self-doubt.

In order to overcome a setback, tools are required to process big emotions like that of failure to achieve a goal. Putting yourself in her position, circle yes or no in the following questions or answer them in your head.

1. Would you have quit when the fog set in? Yes No

2. Would you have taken a break from swimming after realizing you were just one mile away from your goal? Yes No

3. Would you train and try again? Yes No

Reflecting on your answers, ask yourself which tools you have to help you get through big emotional setbacks that do not involve self-sabotage. Record any thoughts in the space provided or in a journal.

_____

_____

_____

_____

_____

_____

_____

_____

Florence Chadwick did not let self-doubt defeat her a second time. She decided to attempt the swim again only two months after her failed attempt, and this time, the same thing happened. The fog settled in. But not everything was the same as the first swim. This time, Florence was different. She had developed self-confidence and bravery and made a conscious decision not to allow her mind to defeat her. Instead, she imagined the shores of Catalina Island and kept swimming. After more than 16 hours, she made it and became the first woman ever to complete the swim! For good measure, she decided to do the same swim twice more, proving to herself that she can accomplish whatever she sets her mind to and modeling for all other women that they are capable, they are brave, they are strong, and they are worthy (Maccarone, 2018).

The next time you find yourself in need of a little perspective, ponder the things below:

- Ask yourself: Is it true? Is it kind? Is it necessary?

- Take three or more deep calming breaths.

- Ask yourself: What are other possibilities?

- If in an argument, tell the other person you need a moment to gather your thoughts.

- Ask the other person to repeat their point of view so you can understand.

- Ask yourself: What can I learn from this?

- Ask yourself: How would you prefer someone to react if they disagreed with your opinion?

- Take time for yourself. Draw, write, or go for a walk.

- Zoom out, but don't zone out.

The Girl and Her Horse

This is a *once upon a time* sort of story about a girl named Josie who loved horses more than anything else in this world. Josie read books about horses, had puzzles, photos, posters, stuffies, figurines, and shelves full of horse books. She dreamed of one day having a horse of her own, but until then, her horse would always be Zola, the beautiful brown horse with the deep dark eyes that lived on the farm down the road. The family who owned the horses told Josie she and her friends were always welcome.

Josie had been teaching Zola how to pick things up on her own, how to give kisses, and other tricks she couldn't wait to show off to her friends. She had it all planned out and invited her two best friends to come hang out after school. When they got to the farm, Zola wasn't in her usual spot near the apple trees. Josie walked into the stables and found Zola sleeping.

"Come on ZoZo," Josie called. "Let's show everyone your tricks."

Zola opened her eyes but didn't want to get up.

"Come on ZoZo," Josie said.

Zola reluctantly got up and followed Josie out into the field. When they got there though, Zola laid back down.

Josie's friends were unimpressed and teased her about Zola being lazy and not actually knowing any tricks. Frustrated, Josie hollered at Zola to go back to the stable if she wanted to sleep, but Zola didn't move a muscle. She just closed her eyes. Josie walked home with her friends and endured the teasing until they went home.

Josie didn't go to see Zola until the next day when she noticed Zola limping. Josie rushed over to check on her and saw a sharp rock lodged under her horseshoe. She gasped and immediately pulled the stone out and when she did, Zola stood up and nickered happily.

"I'm so sorry, girl. I was mad at you for ignoring me in front of my friends yesterday. I didn't even think to check you over for pain. I'm sorry, ZoZo."

* * * *

We all experience pain we cannot see. Whether it be physical, emotional, or mental, unseen pain is sometimes worse than obvious suffering. If someone has just broken their leg, you are not going to be mad at them if they scream or do not have patience or are a little grumpy. If someone has the flu and vomits in the school bathroom, though probably super grossed out, you'd feel sorry for them and offer to help.

On the other hand, if someone slams their locker shut, storms off, bumps into you and spills orange juice all over your shirt, you'd probably holler or tell them to watch where they're going, and you'd probably feel annoyed and angry. But what you didn't know is that that person just got off the phone with their social worker and found out they are being placed in a different foster home than their sibling. If you knew this person's story, the spilled juice wouldn't seem so bad, and you would likely react by telling them not to worry about it and that you were so sorry to hear about their situation.

Perspective can make the difference between positive and negative, hurting and healing.

Journal Prompts

Journaling has scientifically proven benefits for people of all ages. Writing freely or responding to a prompt brings the mind into awareness and increases happiness. According to Milne (2019), journaling helps you to learn more about yourself, to become more aware of your emotions and reactions, to notice sensations in the body and where they come from. This practice can also increase your awareness and compassion for others. The more you read and write, the more you learn, the more confidence you gain, the higher you perform academically and socially.

Writers work through problems and challenges and can open the mind to other perspectives while also increasing their memory and ability to communicate clearly. Journaling gives you the space to be completely honest with yourself and to say things you otherwise would hold in. Journaling can be a way of healing and moving forward with self-compassion. Begin by writing whatever is on your mind or feel free to reflect on the following questions.

Can you remember a time when you unintentionally hurt someone's feelings because of an invisible pain you were experiencing at the time?

_____

_____

_____

_____

_____

_____

_____

1. The next time you get into a disagreement with someone, what can you remind yourself of before the situation escalates?

    *Clarify before assuming another person's intent.

    *_____.

    *_____.

    *_____.

    *Remind yourself that everyone has good days and bad.

2. Make a list of affirmations you can say to yourself when self-doubt inevitably creeps in.

- I am _____.

- I am worthy.

- I am capable.

- I am _____.

- I am _____.

- I can do hard things.

- I am brave.

- I am _____.

- I am enough.

3. Reflecting on your experiences, ask yourself if your perspective has changed over time. Have you had a painful experience that you can now see how you've grown because of that unexpected event?

I invite you to record in a personal journal or in the chart below your experiences for a visual tool to see your growth with the aim of boosting self-confidence and compassion. Don't worry if you are not ready to record your experiences. It's okay if none comes to mind. You can always come back to this when it feels right.

The event: _____

Thoughts and feelings at the time:

_____

_____

How this has impacted your life:

_____

_____

Thoughts and feelings now:

_____

_____

The event: _____

Thoughts and feelings at the time:

_____

_____

How this has impacted your life:

_____

_____

Thoughts and feelings now:

_____

_____

Chapter 5: Making Decisions

Life is very interesting... in the end, some of your greatest pains become your greatest strengths. –Drew Barrymore

Spend some time in your mind for a moment. Allow your thoughts to come and go, change and morph, float by slowly. Then, gently bring your attention to your breath. Take one big inhale through the nose. Hold, 1, 2, 3. Exhale through the mouth with a sigh. Follow the exhale as far as you can before resuming your natural rhythm of breath.

Ponder the above quote. Think about what it means to you and notice what sort of feelings it evokes. Write your thoughts in a journal.

_____

_____

_____

_____

_____

_____

Share the quote with trusted friends and family members to get their perspectives. Hearing the opinions and experiences of others is vital to building empathy, increasing compassion, and supporting personal growth. Record their ideas.

_____

_____

_____

_____

_____

_____

_____

_____

_____

_____

_____

_____

_____

_____

_____

_____

_____

_____

_____

_____

Will You Live Their Dream or Yours?

Being a teenager is confusing and full of internal turmoil as you navigate changes in your body, friendships, family, interests, etc. Thus far, most major decisions have been made for you, like where you go to school, the kind of home you live in, the food you eat, when and where you go to sleep, the family you are or are not connected with, and so on. Yet, on the other hand, once you reach your second to last year of high school, you are expected to figure out what you want to do with your life. I also think that sometimes adults forget to remind you that you do not have to choose just one thing to dedicate your life to.

For some people, the idea of building a career in their passion or following the family legacy provides great pride and comfort in knowing they will succeed because of the immense support surrounding them. For others, the idea of staying home after high school could feel like a prison in which they feel trapped and no longer see themselves fitting in. In your personal journal, reflect on your future aspirations. Consider these questions to drive your reflection:

1. What does your family advise?

2. How does that compare to what you think and feel?

3. If you had the privilege of choosing anything you wanted, what would that be?

4. What is most important to you?

Medicine or Music

Mia is in the 12th grade and has some tough decisions to make. She is torn between what she wants and what her parents want. Her whole family is made up of doctors and other professionals in the medical field, but Mia's passion is music. She applied to pre-med programs per her parents request, but she also applied to a prestigious music school without their knowledge, and to her delight, she received an acceptance letter to her dream school.

Mia was worried. She worried about telling her parents, about disappointing them, and about whether or not she would make it as a musician. She wasn't sure which road to choose. Her mind said to be a doctor, and her heart called out to music. She spent countless hours practicing her music and talking with friends and teachers about her dilemma, trying to decide what to do.

All everyone ever said was, "Do whatever makes you happy." It sounded simple, but it wasn't. It was tradition for everyone in Mia's family to follow the path into medicine, and she couldn't bear the thought of disappointing them. She knew she would have the support of her friends and teachers no matter her decision, but she didn't think her parents would support anything other than pre-med.

Eventually, after weeks of deliberation, Mia decided to talk with her parents about how she felt, that she wanted to follow her passion and accept admittance to the music school. Initially, Mia's parents were worried and couldn't believe she thought music would finance her life, but they shared their concerns openly, as did Mia. In the end, Mia decided to attempt both. On one hand, her parents made a good point about medicine being guaranteed income and financial security, but on the other hand, music was her passion and her dream.

Mia accepted entrance to the music school but requested that it be dropped to part-time. Luckily, she was accepted to the pre-med school nearby as well and took a few classes a week. She and her parents agreed that passion is just as important as security. Together, they came up with a plan to attempt both for one year and by the end of that year to reassess the situation.

Mia felt confident in her decision. She knew deep down that advice shared by those with more life experience should be considered as well as where her heart called. She ended up finishing music school first, played in a local orchestra, and offered instructional classes while working toward her medical degree.

Powerless or Powerful

Ava is going through a difficult time in her life. She has experienced bullying, the loss of all of her grandparents, and the loss of her dad. Her boyfriend of three years broke up with her and immediately began seeing someone else, and now her grades were declining. Her family has begun to question her stability.

Ava often experiences intense feelings of overwhelm and powerlessness. One day, Ava woke to hear her little sister crying in the bathroom, with makeup smudged across her face. Ava helped her sister wash her face and listened as she spoke about kids at school calling her a baby, telling her she was ugly and stupid. She spoke about missing their dad and feeling like she wasn't doing enough to help out.

Ava's little sister mirrored many of the feelings Ava had about herself. In that moment, Ava decided not to allow either of them to continue living in such despair. She found the inner strength to turn her pain into motivation. She began focusing on self-care and included her sister as well. While Ava found solace in writing poetry, her sister found confidence through dance. Both girls shared their passions with each other and encouraged each other to join the writing club and dance team at school.

As they pursued their passions and expressed their feelings, they became more confident in themselves. Ava began performing her poetry at open-mic events for teens at the local cafe, and her sister was recruited to the city dance academy. These girls, who had already gone through so much in their young lives, were able to adjust their perspective, gain a new mindset, and find light within the dark.

Tips for Regaining a Sense of Power

In all honesty, numerous things are beyond our control and can leave us with a sense of powerlessness, like your family moving across the county, traumatic events you were exposed to or a part of, or the age at which you must begin to work. Before continuing through this section, write or think about the things in your life that have made you feel powerless. Draw or write in your journal.

The Power of Choice

While a person may not have a choice in what happened to them or even what's happening around them, they always have a choice in how they react and how they move forward. Sometimes, when something awful happens to us, we are engulfed in a cloud of self-pity and self-deprecation; other times, we are enraged. If we're not careful, the horrible thing that we experienced can quickly become our identity, the story we always tell, crutch we use to explain away poor decision-making, or lack of motivation (Chopra, n.d.).

For example, in the above story about Mia, we saw that she had two choices: to follow her parents' dream or her own. Mia could have followed in her parents' footsteps in order to please them. If she had done this, she would likely resent her parents, and she may use them and the pressure she felt as the reason she didn't get to pursue her dream. She could have easily painted herself as a victim of being forced into a life she didn't want. Others who saw Mia's musical talent could have aided in this image of her being a victim by reassuring Mia that she was too talented to throw her skills away the way she did. Mia could have chosen a life that was never meant for her all just to please someone else. However, Mia overcame her feeling of powerlessness by realizing and accepting the choice she had to make. Rather than allowing that feeling of helplessness to overtake her, Mia chose to follow her heart, and her life panned out the way she had hoped.

In the story about Ava and her sister, both girls had experienced multiple emotional traumas that severely impacted their lives. They could have chosen to allow those losses to dampen their sense of self, they could have chosen to let the bullies win by believing the words they said, and they could have used their losses as excuses for not completing schoolwork, attending events, or participating in extracurricular activities, but they didn't. Ava saw what it was doing to her little sister, and the desire for her sister's happiness motivated her to make the choice to bring them up out of the darkness. Rather than choosing to allow difficult emotions to keep them down, they used them as motivation to go forward, to find their passions, and to learn more about themselves.

Going back to the events you listed about your own life, can you see any choices you may have? What do you need in order to move through this difficult time?

Stop Giving Your Power Away

Becoming powerless and developing a feeling of helplessness does not happen overnight; it happens over time, often going unnoticed. Some people are happy to relinquish their power and give it away freely. Being powerless is often the key to becoming popular, being accepted, and feeling protected. Before you shut down this idea, claiming that you would never willingly give your power away for free, ask yourself how many times you have stayed quiet out of fear of upsetting someone or saying the wrong thing? How often have you faked interest in something just to fit in with the crowd you wanted at school? Do you adjust how you speak, what you speak about, and with whom you are friends based on perceived opinions of others? Each time you silence yourself, you are giving away your power (Chopra, n.d.).

Each time you allow someone to speak over you, each time you decide that others matter more than you, each time you follow the opinions of the crowd, you are slowly diminishing your self-worth by giving your power to them. Without a sense of self-worth, you cannot regain your sense of power (Chopra, n.d.).

Regain your sense of power by taking some of the actions below:

- Speak your mind.

- Try something new.

- Ask for advice from trusted adults.

- Identify your strengths.

- List your skills.

- Challenge your thinking: Is it true? How do you know?

- List times or moments in which you feel empowered.

- Ask yourself what you could do differently next time.

- What is the actual worst-case scenario?

- Spend more time on your interests and hobbies.

Develop Your Core Self

You might read this and ask, "Who am I if I'm not me?" "What does it mean to develop myself if I'm already me?" Your personality is always evolving and developing based on your experiences. Human beings do not automatically mature. Sure, we grow up and become adults, but unlike animals who instinctively act based on their primal desires, human beings don't always act instinctively. We often allow our instincts to be silenced by others, by worry, by depression, or by society. Whoever your silencer is, find out and consciously make efforts to remind yourself that you are awesome (Chopra, n.d.)!

You can like whatever and whoever you want, you can wear whatever you feel good in, you can try new things, fail, and succeed, and you can be whoever you want to be. The hard part is not allowing outside influence to cloud your decisions. The older you get and the more experiences you have, the more you will come to understand that a life spent worrying about what other people think or about fitting into made-up beauty standards is not a life lived but a sentence served (Chopra, n.d.).

Life is full of change; therefore, it is unrealistic to think that if you like basketball today that you must love it for the rest of your life. Just because you have been best friends with someone for years doesn't mean you must remain friends if you grow apart. If you have lived in the same town your entire life, that doesn't mean you can't move elsewhere someday.

Think about the life you lead right now and make your own chart or record in a personal journal.

Today's date: _____

Things I have to do:

_____

_____

Things I enjoy doing:

_____

_____

_____

Things I wish I could give up & why:

_____

_____

Things I want to try:

_____

_____

_____

Things that I can let go of:

_____

_____

_____

_____

Do It Scared

When I suggest trying new things, I don't mean to go sign up for just anything. What I mean is to try something you're interested in but have been too nervous, shy, or scared to actually try. The key is to look for motivation. Why do you want to try this club, sport, or activity? What is holding you back? What positive feelings or skills will you gain if you try? The very worst thing that will happen is you'll discover something you don't like. In that case, don't sign up again. That's the point of living, to try everything and find out what sparks the joy in you, what makes you light up, and what makes you feel excited, loved, and happy? You won't find those things out for yourself unless you take risks, fail, and keep trying until you succeed.

When I was in my senior year of high school, I tried out for the track team. I didn't really try out though; I went to a very small school, and all you had to do to make the team was sign up and show up for practice. I had never taken an interest in running, and to be honest, I still despise it, but at the time, there was a cute boy on the team, and I wanted to spend more time around him. I figured, *it's just running. How hard can it be? I won't be first place, but I definitely won't come in last.*

It turned out that running was hard, I was horrible at it, and I hated it with every fiber of my being, *but* I did meet the love of my life, and we ended up getting married six years later. We've been married 20 years now, and we still joke about my pitiful attempt to be closer to him. I still don't run, but if I hadn't joined the track team, chances are I would be leading a very different life right now.

You never know what unexpected surprises await on the other side of fear. Don't wait until you *feel* ready, because it's entirely possible that you'll never feel ready. Do it anyway!

Those of you on Instagram and TikTok might have heard of Elyse Myers. She is a content creator normalizing life with anxiety. Her advice comes from a tip she offered to Nike for a new campaign: "Just do it scared, anxious, tired, overwhelmed." Just do it anyway, a slogan for normal people, not just athletes. For people who generally feel worried or overwhelmed by seemingly minor tasks, "Just do it scared" applies to so many things that we might otherwise avoid (Myers, 2022).

What are three things you would do if you weren't choosing to let fear hold you back?

1. _____
   _____
   _____

2. _____
   _____
   _____

3. _____
   _____
   _____

Chapter 6: Relationships

It's better to be yourself and have no friends than to be like your friends and have no self. –Unknown

I heard this the other day and thought it would be thought-provoking to include here for you to read. If you choose to be fully, 100% yourself and lose your friends, were they ever truly your friends to begin with? If you choose to alter yourself to fit in with your friends, are you living a lie? Perhaps you think it's okay to bend a little bit to fit in, or maybe you think it's more complicated than that. No matter your viewpoint, continue throughout this chapter to learn to spot the differences between a healthy friendship and a toxic one. Learn some tools that can help you to set boundaries and build true connections with others.

Below or in a journal, record your thoughts about the quote at the beginning of the chapter.

_____

_____

_____

_____

Healthy Relationships

*Female friendships that work are relationships in which women help
each other belong to themselves.* –Lousie Bernikow

Though this quote is specific to women, it can be adjusted to
fit people of all genders. True friends want you to be yourself,
they want you to embrace everything that makes you you
because you are the person they love, the person they choose
to spend their time with. A good friend celebrates your highs
and supports you through your lows.

Besties and Battles

Winnie and Olive have been best friends since they were in the
first grade. They've been in the same class more years than not,
they've done everything with each other and shared their
biggest secrets in confidence. However, when they started high
school, they were faced with a conflict so big it tested the
validity of their friendship.

Winnie joined the cheerleading squad and became more
involved in school activities like yearbook, student council, and
book buddies, while Olive became more involved in art and
joined the school's art club. Their schedules no longer mirror
each other, and they begin to spend less time together as the
year progresses.

One day, Winnie accidentally posted a photo online that reveals Olive's secret passion for sculpture. Olive saw the post right after school and was upset and felt betrayed by her best friend. The two girls got into a huge fight and stopped speaking to each other.

Winnie apologized profusely, but Olive did not believe for one second that posting a photo of her most recent sculptures to be a mistake. Days turned into weeks, and the besties did not speak to each other. It was the longest they'd gone without speaking since they met.

Both went through the days attending their different clubs, hanging out with friends they've met through new interests, but Winnie felt an emptiness in the spot where Olive remained for so long. She decided to reach out and apologize for posting the photo and for lying about it.

Olive hesitated to accept the apology but agreed to talk things out. She was mad, but she missed Winnie too. They met after school at their favorite coffee shop, and both ordered the same thing they've ordered since their parents started letting them go alone back when they were 13: hot chocolate and a brownie.

The girls spent over an hour having an honest conversation about their feelings. Olive was able to understand that Winnie betrayed her trust because she was proud of her not because she wanted to reveal her secret. Winnie understood why Olive was hurt and promised not to post anything without her approval going forward.

They realized they didn't want their differences and new interests to break up their friendship. They found a way to work time together into their schedules and find ways to support each other's new interests. Winnie and Olive know that their friendship is stronger than one conflict and that they will always be there for each other, no matter what. Since this conversation, Winnie and Olive's friendship has never been stronger. They've reached a new level in knowing that their love for each other is worth facing challenges together and finding ways to understand one another.

Qualities of a Healthy Relationship

Whether you are exposed to healthy relationships or not, it is beneficial to listen to those who have experience, to read about self-love, to know that you are worthy of respect, love, safety, and companionship. No matter what goes on around you, your worth does not change. The following list is a good start for what to seek in a relationship both with yourself and with others. If you feel any relationship you have does not meet many or any of these requirements, ask yourself if it's a necessary relationship, one that you feel safe communicating your feelings, how else it could be repaired, or if it's time to let go. If at any time you feel unsafe, confide in a trusted friend or adult or go to local authorities for help.

- **Mutual respect:** In a healthy relationship, you will value each other and know each other's needs, hopes, dreams, and boundaries regardless of whether or not you share a similar opinion. You genuinely care about each other and build each other up. Sharing interests, hobbies, lifestyles, values, and goals make building a bond easier, but they are not necessary to building a healthy friendship (Ali, 2019; youth.gov, 2000).

- **Sharing:** When you have a healthy relationship with someone, you want to share news with this person. You have a natural impulse to tell them the good and bad things, the tiny moments and the big ones. Maybe you talk for hours every day, or maybe you share memes on social media after school. No matter what you share or how often you share things, each time, you genuinely believe that whatever you say your friend will want to hear (Ali, 2019).

- **Honesty:** By being truthful, you strengthen your relationship and build trust. Living honestly is a part of living freely. You should feel free and safe to be honest in a healthy relationship. Disagreements are inevitable, and in a healthy friendship, both parties are able to disagree and be considerate, kind, and compassionate toward each other (Ali, 2019; youth.gov, 2000).

- **Being yourself:** You are each able to be completely yourselves and let your guard down. You feel safe, supported, and comfortable expressing yourself. You do not feel the need to change who you are to fit in with this person. You feel accepted, and this makes you love yourself more as well. You don't think twice about sending a double text, telling them an embarrassing secret, or asking to spend time together (Ali, 2019; youth.gov, 2000).

- **Active listening:** You listen to what each other has to say and hold space for that rather than listening while also thinking of ways to respond. Providing a safe space for each other to express thoughts and feelings is vital to building a relationship. When we always think about how to respond, we sometimes take away the opportunity for the other person's full expression. You make time for each other and are there to support each other no matter what (Ali, 2019).

- **Kind communication:** Every relationship will experience conflict and anger at some point. In a healthy relationship, people are able to communicate their feelings without feeling afraid to do so and without hurting the other person. Both people stick to the subject during a disagreement and avoid bringing up other grievances. When the disagreement becomes too much, both are able to take a short break and come back to the discussion with a calm body and an open mind (youth.gov, 2000).

- **Good memories:** One of the best things about having healthy relationships is the happy memories you have and continue to add to. The positive moments greatly outweigh the negative moments (Ali, 2019).

Reflection

Think about the friends, family, romantic, school, work relationships you have. Which of the above traits are within those bonds?

_____

_____

_____

_____

_____

_____

_____

_____

Toxic Relationships

You are not required to set yourself on fire to keep other people warm.

–Joan Crawford

Frenemies

Rory and Madeline were very close friends from the 5th grade all the way until the 10th. When they entered high school, their relationship started to change. Madeline became really worried about what everyone else thought, who liked her, and how she looked. She started projecting this onto Rory.

Madeline became controlling of Rory, telling her what she should be interested in, what she should wear, how she should speak, who she should hang out with. She was jealous if Rory spent time with someone else or when she started getting noticed for her drumming skills. Even though Madeline wasn't accepting of Rory, Rory remained loyal to her friend and continued to spend time with her and listened to her complain and criticize. Their friendship went from listening to music and dancing in their bare feet to daily conflict.

One day, when Rory was practicing drums in the music room at school, a few kids walked in carrying instruments. They all set up near Rory and one-by-one they joined in. The group played music together for a while and when they stopped, the kid playing the guitar asked Rory if she wanted to join their band and start practicing at lunch time.

The next day, instead of going to sit with Madeline in the cafeteria, Rory went to the music room. She ate lunch with her new bandmates, talked about their music tastes, and then played a few songs they all knew. Rory started doing this more often and Madeline did not like it. She started spreading rumors about Rory and even tried to turn their mutual friends against her.

When Rory heard the rumors and noticed their friends starting to whisper behind her back, she felt hurt and betrayed, but she did not sink to Madeline's level. Instead, Rory started noticing how Madeline had changed, how the choices she made were to hurt Rory on purpose. Rory realized the friendship was not worth saving because she knew she deserved to be treated better than that. Rory distanced herself from Madeline and refused to engage in the rumors, she continued joining the band kids in the music room, and she made new friends who accepted her for who she is. The new friends were proud of Rory for standing up for herself and for setting boundaries that wouldn't allow Madeline to hurt her anymore.

Madeline struggled with insecurities, and her negative behavior caused her to lose her best friend. While she went on to deal with these issues alone, Rory followed her passion, enjoyed her new group of friends, and felt like she could be herself without criticism.

Qualities of a Toxic Relationship

Just as there are signs of a healthy relationship, there are plenty for unhealthy or toxic relationships as well. A toxic relationship is one where you lose your sense of self-worth, where you question yourself, feel like you walk on eggshells, or feel unsafe. Relationships are meant to improve our lives and to teach us more about ourselves and humanity. Not every relationship, no matter how long it's been, is worth losing yourself for. Continue reading to learn about some signs a relationship is toxic and unhealthy.

- **Imbalance of give-and-take:** Have you ever watched *Inventing Anna*? The TV show is based on the real life of a woman named Anna Delvy, who conned her friends into giving her money they couldn't afford to lend. She would often promise to pay them back, call them crying and in crisis guilting them into dropping whatever they were doing to go to her rescue. This is a prime example of a toxic friendship: someone who always needs you and demands your time yet never gives anything in return. They do not acknowledge your needs, and your concerns are often met with stories of times deemed worse than yours. While no relationship is always 50/50, in a healthy relationship, there should be a balance of support for each other. When you point this out to the toxic friend, they will behave in a way that paints themselves as a victim and makes you out to be the bad friend rather than try to rectify the issues or apologize (Graybill, 2022; Smith, 2010).

- **Enhanced negative qualities in you:** While change is inevitable, a toxic relationship will not support change that they feel takes you further away from them. For example, you and your friend always attend high school parties where drinking and smoking take place. You begin to notice how this negatively impacts your physical and mental health, so you decide you no longer want to participate in these activities. A healthy friend would support your choices, while a toxic friend would encourage you to remain the same, to continue drinking and smoking with them. Here's another example. If you're having trouble in a romantic relationship, your toxic friend might encourage you to end it immediately without support for working on the issues. If you confide in them your struggles with self-esteem, instead of building you up, a toxic friend would encourage you to change your appearance to fit more into the ideal beauty standards. No matter what you do to try to better yourself, your toxic friend is there to bring you back down (Smith, 2010).

- **Lack of support:** While teasing in any relationship is normal, a friendship or relationship of any kind should support and enhance your mental health, not bring it down. A relationship is deemed toxic if you feel you cannot be yourself without receiving criticism, if you censor yourself and do not speak your mind out of fear. If you leave your interactions with this person feeling bad about yourself, or if you begin to dread or avoid seeing them, it is likely the relationship is unhealthy. When you confide in your friend, they brush off your concerns or share your information with others. If you approach your friend about your feelings of their lack of support for you and are met with more criticism or blame, it is a clear sign to move on as this relationship is not a healthy one to foster (Smith, 2010).

- **No trust:** One of the best parts about having a close friendship and relationship is the ability to share whatever is on your mind in confidence that they will not share anything you request to be kept between you. In a toxic relationship, you lack trust of the other person. You know they cannot keep secrets, they are unreliable, and they may even use this information against you. Of course everyone slips and makes mistakes sometimes, and one slip of a secret isn't grounds for ending a friendship or labeling a relationship as toxic, but if it is a regular occurrence, you can conclude that this person probably isn't someone you want to invest in too deeply (Smith, 2010).

- **Constant disappointment:** Within a toxic relationship, the other person does not consider your needs, boundaries, or desires. For example, if you have a date set for spending time one-on-one where you have voiced the need to confide in them, without notice, this friend will bring other people along and then paint you as the person who is controlling of them not wanting to share their company. This person often disappoints you by not keeping their word, not adhering to plans made, and generally having a disregard for your well-being (Smith, 2010).

- **Loneliness, sadness, and isolation:** Being around friends and loved ones should make you feel happy, comforted, safe, free. You should feel a sense of connection. If you are feeling like this person doesn't value your friendship, it's likely because they don't. As human beings, our feelings, instincts, and emotions exist first and foremost to protect us from harm. I believe that most of the time, our gut feelings are right, and we should not ignore them (Raypole, 2020).

- **Different relationship goals:** A relationship can turn toxic if the friend decides they want something different than you do and is unwilling to move on from this desire. For example, if your close friend decides they want a romantic relationship with you, but you do not share these feelings, they will not be able to let go of the idea that you belong to them. In rare occasions, both parties can come to an agreement as to the definition of the relationship, but in most cases, if one person has feelings that are not reciprocated by the other, this will drive the friendship apart and make it unhealthy for both parties to continue. It may require you to end the friendship (Smith, 2010).

Reflection

Again, considering your friendships and your family, romantic, school, and work relationships, which of the above traits do you see or feel reflected?

_____

_____

_____

_____

_____

_____

_____

_____

_____

_____

_____

_____

_____

_____

_____

Suggestions for Navigating Toxic Relationships

Next, you will find journal prompts and self-reflection questions to help you gain awareness of the impact of your relationships. Feel free to record in this book, in a personal journal, or simply thinking about them for some time. The more we know, the more conscious decisions we can make to build a life of support and joy.

- **Be conscious:** Bring your awareness to how you feel before, during, and after interacting with the person. Ask yourself the following questions:

    1. Do you feel at ease, look forward to seeing them, and have the urge to share and be around them? Yes - No - Sometimes

    2. Do you dread spending time with them, make excuses not to meet up, or feel drained while hanging out and for a time afterward? Yes - No - Sometimes

    3. Why are you friends with this person?

        _____
        _____
        _____
        _____

    4. How might your life look with continued friendship?

        _____
        _____
        _____
        _____
        _____

How might your life change if the friendship ended?

_____

_____

_____

_____

_____

_____

_____

- **Set boundaries:** If you recognize that you may be in an unhealthy relationship but do not feel it is time to end the friendship, be clear about the kind of relationship you want. For example, if this person often puts you down, each time they do this say, "I don't like being made fun of, so if you keep putting me down, we can't hang out anymore." Then, follow through with your words. If they continue to hurt you, walk away (Raypole, 2020).

If your friend values the relationship, they will make a conscious effort to stop, and perhaps the relationship can improve. If they do not value the relationship, they will either brush it off or put you down further by calling you too sensitive or telling you that you can't take a joke. In this case, you should choose to end the relationship before your self-esteem takes greater hits. Everyone is worthy of kindness, compassion, and respect, including you (Raypole, 2020).

- **Open up to others:** Sometimes, when we are caught in a toxic relationship, we unknowingly distance ourselves from our friends. It can be hard to open up to someone you have pushed away, it can be even harder to open up to your mutual friends, especially if you've decided to end the relationship. Chances are that your mutual friends notice the dynamics between you and will be understanding of your decision. You do not need to bad mouth your friend or to give more details than you feel comfortable. Just give a simple, "I decided to end the relationship for my well-being" (Raypole, 2020).

- **Practice self-care:** Ending a significant relationship of any kind has an impact on our lives and on our emotional and physical well-being. If you are going through a breakup of a friendship or romantic relationship, it's important to spend time with people you love. Remind yourself that it is okay to grieve the loss of your friend and that the only timeline for healing you need to follow is your own. Spend time doing things you enjoy, like picking up an old hobby or trying a new one. Make sure to get plenty of rest and spend time outside (Raypole, 2020).

Chapter 7: Your Body, Your Home

Self-care has become a new priority - the revelation that it's perfectly permissible to listen to your body and do what it needs.

–Frances Ryan

The below information is adapted from credible resources with a general overview of teen girl health, combined with my experience as a teen girl, mother, and teacher. If you have any health concerns whatsoever, seek care from your family doctor and confide in a trusted adult.

Listening to Your Body

When it comes to learning about nutrition, health, and body changes, it can be difficult to navigate all of the information out there. It is vital to learn early on that everyone's body is different, and we all experience the same instinctual cues for hunger, rest, movement, and other changes as we grow and mature. You cannot know someone's health just by looking at them. A small body does not equal health any more than a larger body does. It truly is what is inside that counts most. Media, teachers, parents, and peers can all impact how we see ourselves and our health. By practicing mindfulness and by paying attention to our emotions and body cues, we can ensure our own health and become advocates for what we need. Everyone's needs change; everyone's body changes. Health comes in all shapes and sizes (Alexis, 2022).

Nutrition

What is your typical response to hunger? Do you eat something? Do you have a voice in your mind or a parent or friend telling you to drink water instead? When I was little, I had a voice that told me to drink water first, that if I ate anything I would gain weight and be undesirable. This is the narrative the media fed the world in which I lived as a teen girl, and my parents believed this as well. It wasn't until I was well into my adult years that I actually listened to my body instead of everyone else.

If this is what your voice says, quickly begin by changing the phrases, whether you believe them right now or not. Some that helped me are below:

I trust my body.

Food fuels my body and my mind.

Food helps me feel my best.

Food is to be enjoyed, appreciated, and shared.

My body deserves to be nourished.

I love my body.

How you speak to yourself has a massive impact on your physical and mental health. Awareness of your inner dialogue allows you to find freedom in nutrition. While your parents may be the ones purchasing the food in the household and determining what you can and cannot eat, you are able to use your voice. Request to be a part of the shopping or making the grocery list. Be vocal about the foods you enjoy, try everything once, and eat a balanced diet (Alexis, 2022).

A balanced diet includes all foods and does not label food as good or bad. There's no such thing as bad foods, unless you have an allergy, then yeah, don't eat what you're allergic to; otherwise, food is to be enjoyed. Some are high in nutrients and some are low, some provide quick energy, some provide lasting energy, and others provide none. It is your responsibility, privilege, and right to listen to your body cues, notice how foods make you feel, and make conscious choices that make your mind, body, and soul happy.

When you buy into the narrative of good and bad foods, you can fall into the trap of food restriction by which you deny yourself certain foods, attach guilt or shame to eating them, and cause yourself to binge on these foods when they are available. Fruits, vegetables, grains, proteins, dairy, as well as foods like chips, cookies, cakes, and candies all have a place in a balanced diet. It is when we accept food as food and not a reward, punishment, or thing to fear that we will feel even freer in life. Everybody needs sustenance, and there doesn't have to be shame or anxiety associated (Alexis, 2022; Castle, 2021).

Gaining food freedom promotes positive body image and healthy eating attitudes rather than focusing on restriction and weight. Notice how your body feels when eating anything. Some foods give you feelings of energy while others slow you down. Neither is bad, it all depends on you and what you need in that moment. Some people find it beneficial to keep a food-mood journal by which you notice what your body likes and dislikes and how your mood changes with certain foods; however, others may find this triggers negative body image. Whatever your mindset, it is important to communicate any concerns with health professionals and trusted adults (Alexis, 2022).

Below are a few more affirmations to help you remember that eating from all food groups is vital for health and to develop a positive relationship with food:

Food is not a reward or a punishment; it is sustenance for my body.

I prioritize self-care by feeding my body nutritious and delicious foods.

I am in control of my food choices.

My worth is not determined by my food choices.

According to John Hopkins Medicine, everybody needs a different amount of calories to function at its best. Instead of counting calories, ensure that you listen to your body cues. Is it 10:00 a.m and you are feeling grumpy and irritable? Ask yourself, *Have I eaten? Have I gotten enough sleep? When was the last time I drank some water?* Oftentimes, our moods are associated by the amount of fuel, rest, and movement our body has had (John Hopkins Medicine, 2015).

Enjoying foods from all food groups supports growth and development, strengthens your bones, and improves mental health by reducing risk of anxiety and depression. As a result, relationships with the self and others will improve. With a healthy eating habit and mindset, you will notice increased academic performance and a stronger immune system, which reduces your risk of illness and infection (John Hopkins Medicine, 2015).

The following tips include helpful reminders as to what a growing body needs to function at its best (Government of Canada, 2018; John Hopkins Medicine, 2015):

- Eat three balanced meals per day with snacks in between. Include protein, fiber, dairy, fruits, and vegetables.

- Drink water.

- Eat breakfast to kick-start your metabolism and gain energy for the morning.

- Eat without distraction. For example, do not eat every meal in front of a screen or on the go.

- Pay attention to the five senses while eating to help you stay in tune with your body's hunger cues, to be present, and to enjoy the food and eating experience.

- If you feel hungry, eat something.

- Plan your meals, when possible, to ensure proper nutrition. For example, "eat the rainbow" by eating foods of various colors in one meal setting.

- Find joy in preparing meals for yourself and your family or friends.

- Eat your meals with others.

Food is a huge part of culture, so do not deny yourself something you enjoy just because of someone else's opinion about it. Food is fuel, food is love, food brings people together, and food keeps you alive (Alexis, 2022).

Going forward, I encourage you to make note of meals and foods you really enjoy, foods or dishes you'd like to try, and at least one new dish you'd like to learn how to make on your own. Bake, cook, follow a recipe, or make it up as you go along. I invite you to find joy in food.

Sleep

The Center for Disease Control and Prevention states that a person between the ages of 13–18 needs between 8–10 hours of sleep per day. How old are you? Are you getting enough sleep each night? Begin to notice your moods in correlation with the amount of sleep you get.

Romey's Story

Romey is in high school, she's almost 18, and lately she hasn't been sleeping. Romey worries a lot about her grades, what she plans to do after high school, how her friends see her, and if she'll ever love and be loved. Her parents also put a lot of pressure on her to succeed by constantly reminding her that she'll be moving out in 2 years and that she'd better find a job and a career that will support her lifestyle, because once she's of age, she's out.

It's not that Romey's parents aren't supportive or that they don't love her, they do, it's just that they are unaware of the negative impact their words have on their daughter. Not everyone is conscious of how their actions and words impact others. Romey was taught from a young age that she should be the quiet, good little girl who didn't bother anyone or cause any trouble. This pressure had weighed on Romey for what felt like her whole life and now that her 18th birthday was coming up soon, she was scared.

Romey spent her nights studying, researching, snacking, watching TV, and scrolling on her phone. She just could not sleep and felt the urge to fill time. *If I keep working, if I fail, no one will be able to say I didn't try my best,* she thought. No one noticed Romey's lack of sleep until a few weeks went by and they noticed she didn't seem like herself.

She began having trouble concentrating in school, so even though she studied all the time, her grades began to decline because she was too tired to focus. Romey was moody and irritable, and she started causing conflicts with her friends and family. She was overwhelmed, anxious, and unable to make decisions. Romey began to get headaches every day and seemed to catch every illness that ran through her school.

One morning, when her mom went to wake her for school, Romey didn't respond in her usual way with a grunt or a simple *yeah, morning Mom* reply, instead she burst into tears and buried her face into her pillow, turning her back to her mom. Caught off guard, Romey's mom just stood there for a moment before gently sitting on the bed next to her daughter.

Romey opened up to her mom and told her how she was feeling, that she wasn't sleeping and didn't know what to do. While her mom was initially defensive, by the end of their conversation, they were looking up sleeping tips together and scheduled an appointment with the school guidance counselor to help Romey learn tools to cope with anxiety and how to get a restful night's sleep.

* * * *

Tips for getting a good sleep

- **Schedule and routine:** I know it's not always easy to go to bed at the same time or wake up at the same time each day; however, the more consistent your sleep patterns, the better for your overall health. The time in which you must wake up to start your day varies for everyone, thus so will their sleep schedules. If you have to get up at 6:00 a.m. throughout the week, your ideal time to be asleep would be between 8:00 p.m. and 10:00 p.m., whereas if you don't need to wake up until 7:00 a.m., you would want to be asleep between 9:00 p.m. and 11:00 p.m. (CDC Healthy Schools, 2020).

- **Turn out the lights:** Conditions for getting a good night's sleep and finding ease in falling asleep can be related to brightness. To ensure you sleep well, have your bedroom be quiet, dark, relaxing, and at a comfortable temperature if that is something you have the privilege of controlling (CDC, 2016).

- **Limit screen-time:** The human mind is always at work and even more so when we are watching TV, scrolling on our phones, working on computers, or playing video games. It is no surprise that the more we use electronic devices before bed, the more difficult it will be to sleep. Try to turn off your screens before getting into bed at night or at least for a minimum of

30 minutes prior to attempting to fall asleep (CDC Healthy Schools, 2020; CDC, 2016).

- **Avoid large meals before bedtime:** There's nothing wrong with a light bedtime snack, but if you eat a huge meal then try to go to sleep, it is likely that your body will feel uncomfortable, and this will negatively impact the benefits and quality of your sleep (CDC, 2016).

- **Give yourself permission to rest:** No one can be their best selves on lack of sleep. Give yourself permission to rest when you need to rest and move when you need to move. Listen to your body.

Physical Activity

It is recommended that people between the ages of 6 and 17 should do about an hour of moderate to vigorous physical activity per day (CDC, 2020). The key to incorporating movement into your life is finding activities that you enjoy doing. You should move your body because you love it and because you have the privilege to do so, and not because you hate it. Forcing yourself to do exercise you don't enjoy will not result in anything but frustration and resistance, so find what you love and do that! Skipping, Hula-Hooping, sports, weight training, dancing, running, yoga… There are so many activities that are fun and accessible to everyone. Find what you love and do more of that!

Physical activity improves brain function, helps build strong bones and muscles, reduces symptoms of anxiety and depression, and reduces the risk of developing serious health conditions. By getting enough movement into your day, you will increase your energy. Physical activity, sleep, and nutrition all work together to help us function at our best, so pay attention to your body cues, your needs, and your mind (CDC, 2020).

Puberty

When I was a kid, no one talked to me about my body except to tell me that it would change. My mom showed me how to put a pad on my underwear when I started my first period. I also grew up in a time when it wasn't the norm for people to have computers or cell phones, so the only puberty advice I had was from television shows and whatever my friends told me.

Change can be exciting but also scary, especially when it's happening in our bodies where no one sees *and* outwardly for everyone to see. I experienced the intense jump from feeling to feeling, sometimes triggered by seemingly tiny events. Being a teen is hard even for the ones who make it look easy.

Technically speaking, puberty is your body changing from child to adult for the sake of reproduction. Your hormones are constantly changing and sending messages to your body and your mind. You could be happy and excited one minute and riddled with anxiety the next. One day, you are super confident, and the next you want to hide away. You are not going crazy; you are going through puberty, and everyone goes through it. Puberty is not shameful; it is natural (WebMD, 2022).

What to Expect

- **Increase in height and weight:** While everyone grows at different rates, typically, girls will grow the fastest in the months leading up to their first period. You may start to notice that you fill out your clothes more, your pants get too short, or your shoes are too small. You may notice that your hips grow a bit wider and rounder, and body fat increases along the arms, thighs, and upper back. Not to worry, this is completely natural and happens to everyone. Embrace the growth and learn to love your body for what it does for you (WebMD, 2022).

- **Breast development:** Everyone's breasts will grow at different rates. This can happen before the age of nine in some girls and later in others. Budding, or breast growth usually occurs in the early stages of puberty and is when you notice growth under the nipple. Some people find this itchy or a bit tender, and sometimes one grows faster than the other. The area around the nipple will also darken in color. This is normal. Some girls choose to wear bras while others go free. Do whatever feels comfortable and confident for you. It is typically around the age of 12 that you will notice more growth (Goldman, 2015; WebMD, 2022).

- **Hair growth:** You will begin to notice hair growing on your arms, armpits, legs, and around your pubic area. Your uterus will grow, and pubic hair will start to grow on the lips of the vulva. By the time you reach the age of 12 (earlier or later for some people), the pubic hair will grow thicker and get curlier. Some cultures pressure women to remove hair on their bodies, while other cultures embrace it. It is your body, and you decide how you want to present it and protect it (Goldman, 2015).

- **Acne:** Usually around the tween years is when acne can begin to form on the face and back. Keeping good hygiene and nutrition will help to keep the skin clean and clear. Some people grow out of acne, and some people have it into adulthood. Embrace the skin you're in, knowing that everyone has acne sometimes (Goldman, 2015).

- **Your Period:** Also known as menstruation, your period is when your body sheds the blood and tissue that line your uterus. It flows from there through your cervix and out of your body through the vagina. Your hormone levels change throughout each month, often in line with phases of the moon, and will impact your overall feelings and emotions. A typical cycle can last between 24 and 38 days depending on your body and the amount of external stress (Office of Women's Health, 2017).

There are many ways to care for your body during your period. Some cultures advise rest and relaxation during the period while others expect you to go on as normal. However, no matter where you are in the world or which culture you've grown up in, period pain is real and is different for every woman. This is not something to fear as there are plenty of natural and medicinal remedies to ease discomfort (Office of Women's Health, 2017).

You may notice you feel cramps or discomfort in your upper thighs, back pain, bloating, nausea, diarrhea, fatigue, cravings, and other sensations you otherwise may not feel when not menstruating. In the days leading up to your period, you may experience irritability, self-criticism, uncomfortableness, or difficult sleeping. Share your feelings with a trusted adult or medical professional and they will be able to assist you along the way as you learn to embrace your womanly cycle (WebMD, 2022).

Before you get your first period or even after you've had it, you should ask about or look into period products. Nowadays, there are so many options from pads and tampons to cups and period underwear. Try them all to find what makes you the most comfortable. Menstruation isn't shameful or dirty; it is a process of cleansing the body.

The Period Party

When I was little, no one talked about periods or puberty or anything really, at least not in my family. Nowadays, I have friends with teen girls throwing menstruation parties to celebrate their first periods (Santilli, 2019). To me, this is amazing. What a wonderful time to live in where the shame of natural bleeding is transformed into a celebration of life. Below is a story as told to me by my friend whose daughter got her first period at the age of 11. She was the first of her friends and extremely worried about it all. This party helped her embrace her body and take pride in the natural changes making her a woman.

It was a Friday morning and Ray, my friend's daughter, had woken up with blood in her panties. Her mom had talked to her a lot about periods and had already shown her how to use a pad, tampon, and menstrual cup, and had provided period underwear for her daughter to have a variety of products to choose from when the time came. Ray wasn't scared when she saw the blood, because she knew what it was. She went to tell her mom, who helped her clean the sheets, and while they talked, Ray mentioned she was feeling uncomfortable and really wished she could stay home from school.

Her mom let her stay home and suggested she invite her girlfriends over for dinner and a movie. Ray beamed at the idea.

The whole morning, Ray and her mom baked red velvet cupcakes, made red Jell-O, hung red and pink heart streamers, and rented a movie for the girls to watch. Ray had been texting with her girlfriends all day. She decided to name her period Dot, since a period used in punctuation looks like a dot. She thought is was a funny play on words.

After school, when all of her friends arrived, they had fun playing board games and hanging out. After dinner, her mom brought out the cake that had "Welcome Dot" spelled out in red frosting. Everyone burst out laughing at the cake when they saw it, and her brothers were so confused.

"Who is Dot?" they asked.

The girls giggled and ate cake while her brothers wondered who in the world Dot was. From then on, Ray referred to her period as Dot, and when her friends got their periods they had parties and named them as well (Santilli, 2019).

Tracking

There are many apps nowadays that help people track their sleep, periods, moods, nutrition, and a variety of other things.

Some people choose to do this out of pure interest while others are trying to learn more about their bodies and wanting to make informed choices to improve their moods and overall well-being (Lichterman, 2018).

Tracking your period can help you feel more self-aware and prepared. There are a lot of free apps that can help you understand your cycle and not only the times you bleed. Below is a list compiled by Nast, 2021:

- Flo

- Eve by Glow

- Glow

- Clue

- Spot On

- Your phones note-taking app or a journal

Each of the above options provide a wide range of information from syncing with moon cycles to what symptoms to expect and when. By tracking your emotions, bodily functions, and cravings, you can be more in tune with your body. Tuning in to your body builds self-awareness and enables you to notice patterns associated with mood, body changes, and your menstrual cycle. This can give you the power to know what your body needs and when, which can make the days of navigating school and life just a little bit easier (Nast, 2021).

Stress

According to the World Health Organization, stress can be defined as a type of physical, emotional, or psychological strain or change. Everyone experiences stress to some degree; some people can become overwhelmed with stress and need to seek professional guidance while others are able to manage their stress on their own or with their loved ones (World Health Organization, 2021a).

Below is a story of two girls and how they deal with feelings of stress in their lives.

Mara and Lize were best friends. Mara was naturally organized and focused while Lize struggled to manage various commitments and expectations in her life. One day, their teacher reminded the class of an upcoming exam that would determine a huge percentage of their grade. While both girls felt worried about the exam, Mara was able to make a study plan and this made her feel more prepared, but she noticed that Lize was struggling.

Mara knew that Lize's parents had just announced their separation and that this test was on a subject that Lize was not interested in nor confident about. She noticed her friend came to school the next day wearing the same clothes as the day before, no lunch packed, and dark circles under her eyes from lack of sleep. The stress of Lize's life was too much for her to get a restful sleep.

Luckily, Mara knew her friend well and came to school prepared with a plan to help Lize. When she approached, Lize immediately started asking questions about the content being covered on the test and was holding back tears. Mara put her hands on Lize's shoulders and told her to breathe. Mara led Lize outside where they could have some privacy.

Before Lize could ask another question, Mara hugged her and told her she was sorry she had so much going on. She shared her lunch, talked about what they would do on the weekend after the test had been completed, and tried to take Lize's mind off of the things causing her stress. Once they'd eaten lunch, Mara shared some of her stress-managing strategies with Lize and offered to help her study.

Lize agreed and went to Mara's house after school. Together, the girls studied for the test, took frequent breaks, had snacks, drank water, and joked around with Mara's older brother. When test day arrived, Lize felt a little better. While she didn't ace the test, she did pass, and Mara offered to go with her to meet the guidance counselor to talk about all of the stress she was under.

The two friends continued to support each other, and Lize made it through the year just fine thanks to her friend and to being open-minded and proactive in seeking help.

- **Irritability and increased anger:** Teens and others do not always have the words to express how they're feeling, and it can come out in a variety of ways including irritability and anger. If you notice that yourself or someone in your life has changed their moods, inquire as to why that might be. Finding the source can help you solve the problem (Alvord & Halfond, 2022).

- **Changes in behavior:** One day you pay attention in class, and the next, you're acting out and getting in trouble. Maybe you are very social yet for some reason, you are isolating yourself at home. If you notice a drastic change in your behavior, it could be stress related (Alvord & Halfond, 2022).

- **Trouble sleeping:** When we're stressed, it seems sleep is the first thing to go. Trouble falling asleep, staying asleep, and getting restful sleep are all signs of potential stress factors in our lives. If you're feeling tired all the time and sleeping more often, this is also a sign of stress (Alvord & Halfond, 2022).

- **Neglecting responsibilities:** When your mind is occupied by other factors, it can be hard to stick to routine, remember your responsibilities, or find the drive to do anything at all (Alvord & Halfond, 2022).

- **Eating changes:** Just as poor sleep often goes hand in hand with stress, so do changes in appetite and food cravings (Alvord & Halfond, 2022).

- **Getting sick more often:** Stress can bring on more physical symptoms as well, especially if gone unnoticed. Physical symptoms of stress could include stomach aches, headaches, fatigue, general discomfort, and even signs of depression. Talk to trusted doctors or adults about your physical and mental symptoms for help. We all experience stress and learning from each other is how we go forward (Alvord & Halfond, 2022).

Strategies for Coping with Stress

- **Sleep and proper nutrition:** Surprise, surprise! Sleep and eating are at the top of the list. A car cannot function on an empty tank, and neither should you. Take note of your sleep routines and eating patterns and ask for help to regulate them if you are feeling stressed out (Alvord & Halfond, 2022).

- **Exercise:** When we are feeling overwhelmed with stress, it can be really hard to make time for movement, but moving our bodies keeps our mind healthy as well as our body. No one can produce good work or be a good friend when they are stressed out. Take some time to stretch, go for a walk, jump rope, or swim, anything that gets you moving and gives your mind another focus (Alvord & Halfond, 2022).

- **Talk/write it out:** Getting the feelings and thoughts out of your body can be therapeutic and helpful in releasing stress. So, grab your journal or talk to someone you trust and share your worries. Sometimes hearing or seeing them outside of yourself can help you ease stress and gain new perspective (Alvord & Halfond, 2022).

- **Get outside:** Being in nature can reset your mind and give you other things to focus on. Use your senses and go on a walk to refocus your mind. Research has proven that being in nature relieves stress and improves well-being (Alvord & Halfond, 2022).

- **Learn and practice mindfulness:** Mindfulness is being aware of your current state of being and of your surroundings. It is the ability to refocus the mind from what worries you to the present moment that enables you to calm the nervous system (Alvord & Halfond, 2022).

Chapter 8: Mental Health Support

I say if I'm beautiful. I say if I am strong. You will not determine my story - I will. –Amy Schumer

Not only are teenagers growing and changing socially, emotionally, and physically, but the majority of them have spent the last few years limiting social interactions due to the global pandemic. For very formative years, children and teens have spent much of their time at home and not everyone had a safe place to be isolated. This is a collective trauma that seeps into the minds of everyone who's spent the last handful of years worrying about the safety of their very lives. And now, the world has reopened, and you're entering school a completely different person than you were when you were sent to learn from home (World Health Organization, 2021).

Many teenagers have not had traditional experiences like sports events, parties, social engagements that come with schooling and community participation. Making friends is hard enough and now you have to go do that in a body you didn't have before the pandemic. That is a lot to have on your mind and this combined with other life events and experiences have a heavy impact on your mental health.

According to the World Health Organization, 1 in 7 people aged 10-19 experiences mental health struggles, and many of them go without recognition or treatment. Lack of mental health information, social-emotional learning, and combined stigma surrounding seeking help can lead to further social isolation or exclusion, difficulty at school, poor and risky decision-making, and physical health issues (World Health Organization, 2021).

Self-Care

Overwhelmed by the demands of school, friends, and extracurricular activities, Yi doesn't notice her mental health deteriorating and ignores family and friends checking in on her. She insists on powering through and refuses to take a break stating that others have done it, others are doing it, so why can't she?

"Once I finish this year, I'll be golden," she'd say, with tired eyes and a shaking voice.

I need to keep my grades up, excel in my extracurriculars, and land a spot in my dream school overseas, she'd tell herself. *Failure is not an option.*

Yi convinces herself that she is fine even though she's losing sleep, skips meals and opts for energy drinks instead of water, and though she says she has things under control, everyone can see the changes in her demeanor. She's tired all the time, irritable, and experiences anxiety.

Yi says yes to everything partly because she believes she should help others but also because she feels like she has to avoid upsetting or disappointing people. Yi takes on too much and eventually begins to feel depressed, loses interest in things she once enjoyed, and isolates herself from her friends and family.

One day, Yi reaches a breaking point. She has a severe panic attack at school and is rushed to the hospital. While Yi waits for her mom to arrive, a psychologist speaks with her about paying attention to her body cues and the power of the word "no." Yi understands that taking on everything puts her in a mental space where she can't do anything.

Yi started setting boundaries by advocating for her needs. The panic attack changed her perspective, and she started to pay more attention to her body, moods, hunger and sleep cues. By committing to things she was passionate about and by prioritizing her nutrition, sleep, and physical activity, Yi was able to get her grades back up and got into the school she'd be dreaming of.

Not every story of mental health struggles ends like this one. Some people never seek help, some people don't make it out alive. If you or anyone you know is struggling, reach out to trusted adults and qualified professionals who can guide you back to yourself, back into the light.

Tips for Boosting Your Mental Health

- **Foster your connections** with friends and family and let go of unhealthy relationships: Make the people with whom you feel safe, comfortable, and happy a priority and build your own support system. You do not have to share all information about yourself or your feelings, but having people around you who love you and want the best for you helps boost mental health. Make a point to call or see people face-to-face. Tuning into your feelings and using the above chapters to help you understand the difference between healthy and unhealthy relationships can make it very clear who is good for your mental health and who is not. Take back your power by choosing how you allow people to treat you (ChristineXP, 2020; BC Mental Health, 2018).

- **Stay active:** Physical health impacts mental health, which is really hard to remember when your mental health impacts your desire to move your body. Find something you love to do and do that each day, whether it be jumping on a trampoline, walking your dog, playing sports, or practicing yoga (BC Mental Health, 2018).

- **Talk to someone:** Sometimes, people have a lot going on in their minds and bodies and speaking to someone they know about it can be scary or embarrassing. If you feel like you cannot or do not want to reach out to family or friends, try setting an appointment with your school counselor. Look up mental health resources in your community. Confide in someone you trust, seek professional guidance, read books about mental health and the self, or write in a journal. Notice your feelings. Speak or write them out, sit with that feeling, and seek help at any time, knowing that all human beings experience suffering, and you do not have to do that alone (BC Mental Health, 2018).

- **Find something you enjoy:** Reading, sports, art, music, dance, yoga, knitting, writing, creating, animals, and volunteering are some common interests. There are so many awesome things that a person can do and experience in this life. Try everything, find your passion, spend time doing things you love, and notice the increased quality of your mental health (BC Mental Health, 2018).

- **Sleep and eat enough for your growing body:** As a teen under a lot of pressure emotionally, socially, academically, and physically, it is so important that you take care of your mind and body to ensure you live a safe and happy life. You can help make a routine for yourself by setting reminders for sleep times, downloading apps that track your sleep quality (it's actually pretty interesting), turning off your devices before bed, and practicing mindfulness. When it comes to fueling your body, take part in the grocery shopping and meal planning. Find joy in food and food preparation and this will help you nourish your body and soul (ChristineXP, 2020).

- **Make leisure a priority:** We live in a world that is constantly moving and changing, we have technology that is literally attached to our bodies on a daily basis, and we fill our schedules with school and work and activities. There's cooking, cleaning, tidying, and relationships, and on top of all of that, you have to navigate your changing body and think about your future. That is a lot of stuff for anyone! Remind yourself that rest and relaxation are not only incredibly enjoyable, but they are also necessary for balanced mental health (ChristineXP, 2020).

Helping Others

Lily and Grace have been best friends for years, but over the last year, when they both turned 17, Grace has been struggling with low self-esteem and very negative body image. Grace criticizes herself all the time, does not believe compliments told her, and struggles to see any beauty in her body, her mind, or her soul. Grace lives with an overwhelming voice within that tells her she is unworthy of joy.

Lily has always been a positive and confident person, and though she can't understand why Grace sees herself through such a negative lens, she decides that she needs to do more than just listen. Lily has had tough days like anyone else, but she has the ability to keep an optimistic outlook and wants Grace to see the beauty in the world and in herself.

Immediately, Lily begins by pointing out all the things she loves about Grace. Not in a weird, out-of-the-blue overwhelming way, but she makes a conscious effort to remind Grace of her strengths, talents, and beauty.

It's been winter where they are, and they've been inside more often than not, so Lily invites Grace on little adventures to help show her the beautiful things that life has to offer, even when it's freezing outside. Over the next while, they go skating at an outdoor rink and eat lunch at a new restaurant in town. They bundle up and go on a snowshoe walk through the forest with a community group who loans the shoes and provides hot chocolate and tea.

Lily makes sure that the two of them at least go to a coffee shop one day a week after school to help break the routine of getting up in the dark and going home in the dark. They make plans to go to a concert in the spring and recently started learning how to knit scarves.

Over the course of the winter and spring months, Grace begins to adopt a bit of Lily's optimistic outlook. She starts suggesting activities once in a while, smiles more often, and is becoming more self-assured as she finds new interests and forms stronger friendship bonds. Grace begins to talk about their future more often, notices more opportunities, regains a regular sleeping pattern, sees her grades improve, and overall wakes up looking forward to the day rather than wishing to stay in the dark.

Lily's unwavering encouragement and love for Grace helped lift Grace's spirits and improve her mental health. Not everyone has a friend like Lily, but you can be this friend for yourself.

If you are experiencing overwhelming feelings and need help, do not hesitate to tell a trusted friend, adult, physician, psychologist, or call your local helpline. You are not alone, you are worthy, there is a brighter side, and you deserve joy.

A Mindful Practice

I prefer to begin and end meditation practices with a bell or chime. If you have one, sound it now.

Begin by finding a comfortable seated position either on a chair or on the floor.

Settle into your seat and breathe.

Notice the connection between your body and the floor, cushion, or chair.

Notice the weight of your body pressing down.

Roll your shoulders up and back three times before settling comfortably in an upright position.

Bring your attention to the sounds outside of the room.

Next, notice any sounds within your room.

Bring your awareness to your breath.

Pay attention to the feeling of each inhale and exhale.

Do not try to control the breath, simply notice your natural rhythm in this moment.

Inhaling, *I know that I am breathing in.*

Exhaling, *I know that I am breathing out.*

Inhale fully.

Exhale completely.

Follow your breath from the beginning of the inhale, to the middle, to the end.

Notice the brief moment where the breath changes to exhale.

Follow your exhale from beginning, to middle, to end.

As you continue to breathe, imagine waves gently brushing up against the shore.

Ride the waves of your breath, gently flowing in and out with each inhale and exhale.

When you notice your thoughts start to wander, distracted by thoughts, sensations in the body, or sounds.

When this happens, come back to your breath.

Bringing your awareness to each inhale and exhale.

Grounding yourself back in this moment.

Inhaling, *I know that I am breathing in.*

Exhaling, *I know that I am breathing out.*

Bring your attention to where you feel the breath.

The tip of your nose, the belly or chest rising and falling.

Notice the sensations in your body as you breathe.

If you are comfortable, place one hand over your belly and the other over your heart.

Breathe.

Notice the connection between your hands and your body.

Notice the rise and fall as you inhale and exhale.

Say to yourself:

I inhale peace.

I exhale joy.

Breathe.

Stay here for the remainder of the practice or for as long as you feel comfortable, just breathing and being here in this moment. You have nowhere to be and nothing else to do. Just breathe (Prasad, 2022).

Chapter 9: Social Media and Peer Pressure

You can't eat beauty, it doesn't sustain you. What is fundamentally beautiful is compassion, for yourself and those around you. That kind of beauty inflames the heart and enchants the soul. –Lupita Nyong'o

In a personal journal, the physical copy of this book, or even just in your mind, reflect on the words above and ask yourself the questions below:

- What is compassion?

  _____

  _____

  _____

  _____

- What images come to mind when you hear the word, compassion?

  _____

  _____

  _____

  _____

- How might a life of compassion look and feel?

_____

_____

_____

_____

The Positive Side

For many, social media is a space to foster connections and create a community of support. In a study conducted in 2022 by the Pew Research Center, a survey of teens between the ages of 13 and 17 showed that 8 in 10 teens reported that social media helped them feel more connected to their friends by knowing more of what's going on in their lives. Furthermore, the same survey found that 71% of teens in this group said they felt social media gave them a place for creativity (Anderson et al., 2022).

While many adults worry about the impact of social media on teenagers today, part of that worry is that they themselves did not grow up in this kind of connected world. They were out riding bikes with friends with no way of being contacted by their parents. Now, parents buy their kids cell phones to keep in touch. The unknown is scary for some, but teens in this particular study saw the positive side of technology connecting them with the world, enabling them to discover more about themselves and explore various interests (Anderson et al., 2022).

The biggest positives included maintaining friendships, building connections, and accessing information. Social media can be especially positive for those experiencing exclusion. Online spaces, when used safely, can be a wonderful way to connect with people of similar interests who may go to a different school or whom you would not know without their social media account. Entertainment and self-expression are provided and encouraged via numerous platforms (Mayo Clinic, 2022).

Social Media Success

Navaeh was an avid social media user. She was 17 years old and had a strong online presence with hundreds of thousands of followers. She was creative and enjoyed sharing content to inspire others to pursue their artistic sides. Navaeh posted daily photos showcasing her photography skills, love of fashion, and interest in nature's patterns.

One day, Navaeh was contacted by a well-known online brand who wanted her to be the face for their latest campaign. Navaeh was so excited for a few minutes before her mom brought her back down to the reality of meeting people online.

"You don't know these people. What are their intentions? What is this product you'll be representing? Do you know their background history? Do you know if they are ethical in their work? Do you know anything about them besides a pretty picture and an invitation with financial incentive?" Her mom riddled her with questions assuming the worst.

Navaeh was annoyed and disheartened that her mom didn't show her support immediately. She was 17 and being asked to be the face of a major campaign that could kick-start a career in fashion and photography. Reluctantly, she let her mom type her reply to the company stating they would get back to them by the end of the week with a decision.

Navaeh and her mom researched the company together, and to Navaeh's benefit, they found that the company was credible, ethically responsible, and represented a good cause by donating much of their profits to various charitable organizations. By the weekend, Navaeh and her mom were at the photoshoot being treated like family.

Navaeh's first paid modeling job was up on social media for everyone to see. She was contacted by a variety of other companies to work with them as a model and a photographer. Social media was the key to Navaeh's success, and with her mom's guidance, she always made sure to learn about a company before agreeing to represent them.

The Negative Side

A common negative perspective among teen girls is having low self-esteem due to body image concerns. If you follow the media of past and present, you will notice a trend in which the only constant is change. One year, Crocs are in, and the next it's Blundstones. Sometimes articles will praise a woman for losing weight while another will have a plus-size model on the cover. There is makeup to both cover up freckles and to draw them on. If it feels like a losing battle, that's because it is. No one will ever live up to the beauty standards carefully chosen by mainstream media. Their goal is to keep you noticing things about your appearance that must change, when the reality is what has to change is your mind (Ehmke, 2022).

Teens with a more positive or optimistic outlook are more able to see the benefits of social media and more equipped to navigate the variety of images and information they take in on a daily basis. Those who may struggle with self-confidence are more likely to experience the negative side of social media where they compare themselves to others, struggle to feel adequate, and worry about being shamed or embarrassed for sharing their interests with the world (Anderson et al., 2022).

Two teen girls of the same age could look at a photo of another teen girl enjoying vacation with her family, but each could experience the image in a different way. One girl could see the photo and think, *That's beautiful. I can't wait to travel someday!* The other girl might see the photo and think, *I wish I looked like her. I wish my family could afford to travel.* Your mindset and what you choose to expose yourself to impacts your self-perception and your world views (Anderson et al., 2022).

Social media use can negatively impact your sleep and seep into other areas of your life rather quickly. High social media use is also associated with heightened feelings of anxiety and depression (Mayo Clinic, 2022).

For anyone using social media sites like Facebook, Instagram, TikTok, or others where people are encouraged to share their lives openly for the world to see and comment on regardless of their knowledge of us or the lives we live, it is vital that you choose what you expose yourself to. Each of these websites has an algorithm that will personalize the information you see, meaning the site will build your feed based on what your data shows (Barnhart, 2021).

For example, even if you are not a person with conservative beliefs, if you click an image or a link about a conservative-supporting viewpoint, the algorithm will remember this and continue to show you posts in support of that view. If you are interested in vegan cooking and you happen to click on a recipe associated with the diet industry, your feed could begin to fill up with weight loss ads. The information we expose ourselves to on a daily basis influences our conscious mind and can penetrate our subconscious, building a belief system that we had no intention of adopting. The more mindfulness we practice, the more conscious we will become of messaging that has a negative influence on our self-perception (Barnhart, 2021; Mayo Clinic, 2022).

If your parents decided to tell you as a child that the sky was pink, you'd have believed what they said until you heard other people say the sky was blue. The more people telling you that the sky was blue, the more likely you would have been to question your belief system. The same works for the information we expose ourselves too. Remember that the goal of your device is to get your attention. The algorithm does this by sending notifications to make you pick up your phone, shows you a video or image that reflects your most recent searches and views, and succeeds in sucking you in to scrolling their content (Barnhart, 2021).

Scientists and health professionals can attest that someone's physical body appearance is not an indicator of their health, but because the diet industry can profit from people believing an unachievable standard is actually achievable, they will continue to try to sell unrealistic lifestyles, types of food, medications, and other things to make you believe happiness is on the other side of changing your body. Advertising, movies, television shows, and representation in media often show one type of body deemed as acceptable and attractive and the opposite as being unhealthy and ugly. Take back control by paying attention to who you follow and the feelings that arise when you see their posts (Barnhart, 2021).

Social Media Take Down

A teen girl named Ruth was an active user of social media just like everyone else her age. Though her parents limited the use of her phone, Ruth enjoyed connecting with friends, classmates, and people around the world online. However, after moving from middle school to high school in a different town, Ruth room found herself the target of cyberbullying by a group of new classmates who created fake profiles to harass her.

These people targeted Ruth for no other reason than she was new, she was smart, she was a crazy talented singer, and they were jealous. They envied her talent, her kindness, and her ability to do what she wanted without worrying what anyone thought. That was, until they got to her. They created profiles pretending to be her and posted horrible things online about other people in the class. They also created other profiles to engage in insulting comments and embarrassing untrue stories.

This impacted Ruth's entire life. While she was once able to find optimism in her days, now all she felt was sadness. She felt isolated and alone because, if she went on social media to connect with friends, she would see the awful things those kids posted about her or from the fake account pretending to be her. Ruth stopped talking to her friends and often stayed in her room. Her grades declined, and she lost her spot as lead singer in the school play.

While Ruth's friends, family, and teachers supported her and tried to help her regain her self-confidence, Ruth didn't complete her high school years as she had intended. The bullying online infiltrated her mind and took over. She no longer sang, she kept her head down, and she avoided any situation that would put her in the limelight.

Your words create lines in people's hearts and minds the way crumpling a piece of paper leaves unsmoothable lines. Once you say something, all the apologies in the world do not take away the impact of the words said. Your words can change someone's entire self and world view. You have the power to build others up or take them down (Ehmke, 2022).

Chapter 10: Grow Into Your Power

The future belongs to those who believe in the beauty of their dreams.

–Eleanor Roosevelt

Take some time to write about your own dreams.

_____

_____

_____

_____

_____

_____

_____

_____

_____

_____

_____

As a teenager, you are always learning about yourself. Your art teacher could introduce you to pottery one day, and you could become obsessed with it, when the day before, you hadn't even thought about it. You could completely hate running, join track, and meet the love of your life. Life is unpredictable, but you have control over your choices and reactions. Growing into your power means embracing who you are at your core without reservation, loving yourself, and knowing you deserve to take up space, be seen, be heard, and be valued (Jantz, 2017).

It is infuriating as a teen to witness many adults make rules for you and then not do as they preach. You may even push back on rules you disagree with because they don't seem to apply to anyone else. Usually, rules are in place to keep you safe and healthy, but sometimes rules are in place to make life easier for someone else. Find your voice and use it with kindness, assertiveness, and compassion. While teens desire connection to their friends, it is common for them to push back against parents and other authority figures as they learn more about their core beliefs, values, and desires. The more our minds develop, the bigger variety of experiences we will have; the more mistakes we make and the more lessons we learn, the closer we will become to being our own true selves (Jantz, 2017).

The Wrong Crowd

It is not uncommon to feel lost at school or in life sometimes. Some people will bounce from group to group in search of belonging while others will embrace their individuality. Janelle couldn't seem to find where she belonged. One week she hung out in the library with the book nerds reading, but she didn't find a genre that held her attention for long. The next week, Janelle hung out with the kids in the gym while she skipped rope, but when those kids learned tricks, Janelle quickly judged her abilities and left for the kids who sat in the back of the cafeteria.

One day, Janelle was invited by a group of older teens to join them outside at lunch. They seemed confident and carefree, so when lunch came around, Janelle grabbed her sandwich and headed outside. The first day, she went with those kids into the woods and skipped the afternoon of school to explore an abandoned house. Janelle was intrigued by the danger and liked the rush she felt from skipping school, something she'd never done before.

Janelle continued hanging out with this crowd even when they started using her as the lookout while they shoplifted or destroyed public property. One day, they convinced Janelle to try to buy alcohol and marijuana from the liquor store with a fake ID. She did it and succeeded. This made her even more popular with the group, and they began to treat her like royalty.

While Janelle enjoyed the thrill of doing something wrong, the night they were chased out of the park by police officers scared her, and she wanted to make a change before she got into more trouble. She was torn between standing up for what she believed in and being loyal to her friends. She worried that if she refused to participate in illegal activities with them that they might banish her from the friend group, and she'd go back to being alone. On the other hand, she could get into serious trouble that would impact her future.

At this point, Janelle was on very thin ice with her family. Her parents were constantly disappointed in her choices and tried talking to her. Her teachers were concerned about her plummeting grades and her future abilities to get into a good school. With the push from her parents and teachers, Janelle decided to leave her friend group. She told them she could no longer participate in anything illegal, and they all reacted as she expected. They laughed at her, ridiculed her, and threatened to rat on her if she told anyone about anything.

Though Janelle was worried, she knew she had the support of her family and teachers. She stood her ground and avoided that group for the remainder of her school years. She joined the newspaper club and fell in love with writing and sharing stories. Through writing, Janelle was able to dive into various groups at school to get stories for the paper and in doing so, she made a good group of friends who encouraged her to follow her dreams.

People who seem like your friends don't always carry your best interests at heart. Building awareness of self and mindfulness of surroundings can aid in making decisions that benefit your well-being and help you thrive (Gregston, 2015).

Own Your Weirdness

There was once a carefree teen girl named Rainbow whom everyone liked to poke fun at. They teased her about her name, her clothing choices, and the way she spoke. They made fun of her music and the way she danced through the halls at school instead of walking with her face in her phone like everyone else. This treatment would tear down many young girls and even cause anxiety or depression, but Rainbow didn't care.

She was taught from a young age that being who she was was a choice and a calling, and that she could change it at will. Her parents were doctors who had followed in their parents' footsteps, but they wanted Rainbow to be whoever and whatever she wanted. They did not want to pressure her the way they were pressured as kids.

Rainbow was free. She never gave up on being herself, and when others teased her or poked fun at her or called her weird, she would smile and dance by moving on to spend time with friends who wanted her to be herself. By the time Rainbow reached her senior year of high school, she was asked by the principal to give a speech at the graduation ceremony.

Rainbow wasn't valedictorian, she hadn't received prestigious awards, and her plan after high school was to work at her cousin's dog grooming business and study philosophy on the side. Rainbow gave her speech and shocked the crowd.

Instead of strolling across the stage in the traditional cap and gown, Rainbow had sewn her own dress and skipped up to the microphone. Before she spoke, she smiled at the crowd, making eye contact with groups of kids pointing and snickering. Though she was nervous to speak in front of that huge crowd, looking past the kids poking fun at her, Rainbow saw the hopeful eyes of the outcasts, the kids who didn't fit in, the kids who didn't have large friend groups, the weird kids. This speech was to uplift them and to teach everyone else a thing or two about being a good human.

Rainbow talked about the benefits of embracing weirdness, explaining that it is because of our individuality that we stand apart from others. She talked about her experiences and her views on life and the universe, and by the end of her speech, even those who had judged her were standing to clap for her.

Rainbow became a role model for students who came after her. Teachers noticed a shift in the dynamics at school with more kids supporting each other and trying new things. Rainbow inspired others to find themselves and to be happy with who they are, weirdness and all.

Conclusion

Girl, you are magic! When you learn to believe in yourself, follow your dreams, and stand up for what you value and believe in, you will feel free—free of the constraints others try to put you in, free from keeping yourself small. Shine bright, be loud, be heard, and advocate for yourself and for others. You can change the world for everyone, for one person, and for yourself.

Your mind is your most powerful tool, and you will see whatever you look for. Pay attention to your inner dialogue and seek help whenever you feel you need it. Keep believing. Keep fighting. Embrace the freedom and joy of being who you already are. Work to create the life you want and deserve. I invite you to keep a journal, to reflect on your daily emotions, activities, interactions, and thoughts. I encourage you to reread what you write every so often and to celebrate all progress noticed.

This book was for you: to empower teen girls, promote self-confidence, educate you on the inner workings of the mind and the power of outside influence, and to help you find independence and build resilience. I hope that you are inspired to embrace who you are, to recognize your worth, pursue your passions, and to stand up for your beliefs. I encourage you to continue along the path of self-discovery and not to let anyone dim your light.

In your journal, record any reflections you have after reading this book. Go back through your notes, flip to sections you'd like to read again, and use this information to empower yourself. Then, share it with others. Encourage your friends to be themselves, to own their individuality rather than hide it. Remind yourself of the power you hold and remind others of their power too. Together we can build a generation of empowered women who help lead the world with empathy, kindness, compassion, and strength in unity.

With the mind being a major focus of this book, below are some recommended apps and websites for mindfulness practices to help you tune in to yourself:

- Headspace

- Calm

- Smiling Mind

- Three Good Things

All of the above apps are user-friendly and provide tips, tools, and practices to incorporate more mindfulness into your life. A few of the apps also offer spaces to record your thoughts, feelings, or pieces of gratitude to help you refocus the mind onto positive things in your life (Klein, 2021).

We call upon our sisters around the world to be brave - to embrace the strength within themselves and realize their full potential.

–Malala Yousafzai

Thank you

I want to personally thank you for purchasing my book!

Lots of love and effort went into the writing process and I hope you have enjoyed it. More importantly, I hope you found something in it that was useful and personal to you.

Before you leave, could I ask a favor? If you found this book helpful at all, please consider leaving a review. It only takes a few minutes and reviews are the very best and easiest way to support independent authors like me.

Reviews also help people, just like you, who are looking for what this book has to offer.

You can be the means of helping others find me and it might be just what they are needing. Consider sending some good out into the universe and leaving me a review! I really appreciate it.

I read every review and look forward to reading yours!

Until next time,

Shannon Cooke

References

Abernethy, A. (2020, August 8). What is Perspective Taking? The Basics & Benefits Explained. *AMP Creative.* https://ampcreative.com/what-is-perspective-taking/

Alder, S. (n.d.). Shannon L. Alder quotes. *Goodreads.* Retrieved February 4, 2023, from https://www.goodreads.com/quotes/469316-when-you-stop-living-your-life-based-on-what-others#:~:text=%E2%80%9CWhen%20you%20stop%20living%20your%20life%20based%20on%20what%20others

Alexis, A. C. (2022, January 12). What Is Food Freedom? Getting Started, Weight Loss, and Tips. *Healthline.* https://www.healthline.com/nutrition/what-is-food-freedom-getting-started-weight-loss-and-tips

Ali, S. (2019, April 12). Is Your Friendship Healthy? *Psychology Today.* https://www.psychologytoday.com/us/blog/modern-mentality/201904/is-your-friendship-healthy

Alvord, M., & Halfond, R. (2022). How to help children and teens manage their stress. *Apa.org.* https://www.apa.org/topics/children/stress

Amanda N. (2022, May 6). 70 inspirational mom self care quotes for awesome moms. *Mumtasticlife.*

https://mumtasticlife.com/70-inspirational-mom-self-care-quotes-for-awesome-moms/

Anderson, M., Vogels, E. A., Perrin, A., & Rainie, L. (2022, November 16). Connection, creativity and drama: Teen life on social media in 2022. *Pew Research Center*. https://www.pewresearch.org/internet/2022/11/16/connection-creativity-and-drama-teen-life-on-social-media-in-2022/

Ashley Stahl [@AshleyStahl]. (2018, March 12). *Tweets* [Twitter profile]. Twitter. https://twitter.com/ashleystahl/status/973317839087132673

Barnhart, B. (2021). Everything you need to know about social media algorithms. *Sprout Social*. https://sproutsocial.com/insights/social-media-algorithms/

Bernikow, L. (n.d.). A quote by Louise Bernikow. *Goodreads*. Retrieved February 6, 2023, from https://www.goodreads.com/quotes/148947-female-friendships-that-work-are-relationships-in-which-women-help

Brown, B. (2019). *BRAVING THE WILDERNESS: the quest for true belonging and the courage to stand alone*. Random House.

Canada's food guide – Healthy eating for teens. (2022, May 3). *Government of Canada.* https://food-guide.canada.ca/en/tips-for-healthy-eating/teens/

Castle, J. (2021, January 15). Food restriction: What controlling food does to kids. *The Nourished Child.* https://thenourishedchild.com/food-restriction-restrictive-feeder/

Characteristics of healthy & unhealthy relationships.. (n.d.). *Youth.gov.* https://youth.gov/youth-topics/teen-dating-violence/characteristics

Cherry, K. (2021, February 20). Attitudes and behavior in psychology. *Verywell Mind.* https://www.verywellmind.com/attitudes-how-they-form-change-shape-behavior-2795897

Cherry, K. (2006, January 4). The role of the conscious mind. *Verywell Mind.* https://www.verywellmind.com/what-is-the-conscious-mind-2794984

Chopra, D. (n.d.). Deepak Chopra: 5 ways to feel less powerless. *Oprah.com.* Retrieved January 30, 2023, from https://www.oprah.com/omagazine/how-to-feel-less-powerless-deepak-chopra

ChristineXP. (2020, February 26). 10 mental health techniques teen should know about. *Discovery Mood & Anxiety Program.* https://discoverymood.com/blog/10-tips-teen-dealing-with-a-mental-health/

Cox, T. (2011, October 10). Brain maturity extends well beyond teen years. *National Public Radio (NPR)*. https://www.npr.org/templates/story/story.php?stor yId=141164708

Cullins, A. (2017, May 17). 7 activities to help your child develop a positive attitude. *Big Life Journal*. https://biglifejournal.com/blogs/blog/children-positive-attitude

Daum, K. (2016, December 1). These 21 quotes by Amy Schumer will make anyone feel fierce and fabulous. *Inc.com*. https://www.inc.com/kevin-daum/these-21-quotes-from-amy-schumer-will-make-anyone-feel-fierce-and-fabulous.html

Dimension, A. (2017, March 29). Here's why seeking external validation will most likely bring you down. *Alternate Dimension*. https://xperiencedimension.wordpress.com/2017/03/29/heres-why-seeking-external-validation-will-most-likely-bring-you-down/

Earle, A. (2019, December 16). Ep 63: Recognizing strengths to help your teen thrive. *Talking to Teens*. https://talkingtoteens.com/podcast/how-to-help-a-teenager-find-themselves/

Einstein, A. (n.d.). Albert Einstein quotes. *BrainyQuote*. Retrieved February 4, 2023, from https://www.brainyquote.com/quotes/albert_einstei

n_130982#:~:text=Albert%20Einstein%20Quotes&t
ext=Please%20enable%20Javascript-

Ehmke, R. (2022, December 6). How using social media affects
teenagers. *Child Mind Institute*.
https://childmind.org/article/how-using-social-
media-affects-teenagers/

Emma. (2020, December 9). 32 Billie Eilish quotes and lyrics
we all need at some point in life. *Our Mindful Life*.
https://www.ourmindfullife.com/billie-eilish-quotes/

Fincher, B. (2021, February 13). Life-changing quotes for
teenage girls. *Confessions of Parenting*.
https://confessionsofparenting.com/quotes-for-
teenage-girls/

Ford, B. (Host). (2019, February 6). Every day is a fresh start,
start the day with a thankful heart [Audio podcast
episode]. In *Self Improvement Daily*.
https://www.selfimprovementdailytips.com/podcast
/every-day-is-a-fresh-start-start-the-day-with-a-
thankful-
heart#:~:text=If%20you%20think%20about%20it

Goldman, R. (2015, December). The stages of puberty:
Development in girls and boys. *Healthline*.
https://www.healthline.com/health/parenting/stages
-of-puberty

Graybill, J. (2022, March 18). Inventing Anna: Portrait of a stylish abuser. *Medium.* https://jackie-graybill.medium.com/inventing-anna-portrait-of-a-stylish-abuser-aa686f6598ea

Gregston, M. (2015, December 10). The wrong crowd. *Parenting Today's Teens.* https://parentingtodaysteens.org/blog/the-wrong-crowd-2/?gclid=Cj0KCQiAofieBhDXARIsAHTTldoh1zUgpwcKE6R-3zKKnGpiJblOa7T3d3QjOWjpEmSt7LFxeQrvt44aAiqNEALw_wcB

Healthy eating during adolescence. (n.d.). *Johns Hopkins Medicine.* https://www.hopkinsmedicine.org/health/wellness-and-prevention/healthy-eating-during-adolescence

Hilliard, J. (2019, July 15). Social media addiction. *Addiction Center.* https://www.addictioncenter.com/drugs/social-media-addiction/

IdleHearts. (n.d.). It's better to be yourself and have no friends. *IdleHearts.* Retrieved February 6, 2023, from https://www.idlehearts.com/3943/its-better-to-be-yourself-and-have-no

Jantz, G. L. (2017, March 2). Teenagers and their quest to find themselves. *Psychology Today.*

https://www.psychologytoday.com/us/blog/hope-relationships/201703/teenagers-and-their-quest-find-themselves

Johnston, R., & Kelly, A. (2017, October 31). The psychology of mirroring. *Imagine Health.* https://imaginehealth.ie/the-psychology-of-mirroring/

Kaling, M.. (n.d.). Mindy Kaling quotes. *Goodreads..* Retrieved February 4, 2023, from https://www.goodreads.com/author/quotes/194416. Mindy_Kaling

Kaur, R. (n.d.). Rupi Kaur quotes. *Quotespedia.* Retrieved February 4, 2023, from https://www.quotespedia.org/authors/r/rupi-kaur/how-you-love-yourself-is-how-you-teach-others-to-love-you-rupi-kaur/

Keys, A. (n.d.). Alicia Keys quote. *Quotefancy.* Retrieved February 4, 2023, from https://quotefancy.com/quote/1271702/Alicia-Keys-Everything-you-want-to-be-you-already-are-You-re-simply-on-the-path-to

Klein, Y. (2021, February 9). Best mindfulness and meditation apps for teens. *Evolve Treatment Centers.* https://evolvetreatment.com/blog/mindfulness-apps-teens/

Lady Gaga. (n.d.). Lady Gaga quotes. *Goodreads*. Retrieved February 4, 2023, from https://www.goodreads.com/quotes/227942-i-used-to-walk-down-the-street-like-i-was

Lichterman, G. (2018, November 25). 4 top reasons women use period tracker apps. *Hormonology*. https://www.myhormonology.com/4-top-reasons-for-period-tracking/

Lizzo. (2019, April 19). Self-care is rooted in self-preservation, not just mimosas and spa days. *NBC News*. https://www.nbcnews.com/think/opinion/self-care-has-be-rooted-self-preservation-not-just-mimosas-ncna993661

Lyness, D. (2018). How can I improve my self-esteem? *Nemours* *TeensHealth*. https://kidshealth.org/en/teens/self-esteem.html

Maccarone, N. (2018, January 17). You're closer than you think — A story about long distance swimmer Florence Chadwick. *Medium*. https://medium.com/emphasis/youre-closer-than-you-think-a-story-about-long-distance-swimmer-florence-chadwick-99f9cf360b9f

Mankiller, W. (n.d.). Wilma Mankiller quotes. *BrainyQuote*. https://www.brainyquote.com/authors/wilma-mankiller-quotes

Mayo Clinic Staff. (2022, February 26). Teens and social media use: What's the impact? *Mayo Clinic.* https://www.mayoclinic.org/healthy-lifestyle/tween-and-teen-health/in-depth/teens-and-social-media-use/art-20474437

Miller, B. (n.d.). (PPT) Inspirational quotes by famous women. *Pdfslide.net.* Retrieved February 6, 2023, from https://pdfslide.net/self-improvement/inspirational-quotes-by-famous-women-58f9d7f126e0e.html?page=21

Milne, A. (2019, October 4). 10 health and well-being perks of journaling for teenagers. *#Slowchathealth.* https://slowchathealth.com/2019/10/04/journaling-perks/

Mindworks Team. (2019, October 29). Lovingkindness Meditation — A aily script. *Mindworks.* https://mindworks.org/blog/lovingkindness-meditation-a-daily-script/

Morales, S. (2021, June 29). Let go of self-doubt. *Jaime Taets.* https://jaimetaets.com/let-go-of-self-doubt/#:~:text=Self%2Ddoubt%3A%20it%20causes%20us

Myers, E. [@elysemeyers]. (2022). Please @Nike for all of us just hanging in there, this would be incred... [TikTok profile]. *TikTok.*

https://www.tiktok.com/@elysemyers/video/71020
41888571542826?lang=en

Nast, C. (2021, January 6). The 10 best period tracking apps to try in 2021. *SELF*. https://www.self.com/story/best-period-tracking-apps

Nature and mental health. (2021, November). *Mind*. https://www.mind.org.uk/information-support/tips-for-everyday-living/nature-and-mental-health/how-nature-benefits-mental-health/

Oprah's words to live by. . (n.d.). *Oprah.com*. Retrieved February 4, 2023, from https://www.oprah.com/omagazine/oprahs-words-to-live-by-higher-calling#:~:text=I%20know%20for%20sure%20that

Peer, M. (2019, June 6). The differences between your conscious and subconscious mind. *Marisa Peer*. https://marisapeer.com/the-differences-between-your-conscious-and-subconscious-mind/

Physical activity facts. (2022, July 26). . *Centers for Disease Control and Prevention*. https://www.cdc.gov/healthyschools/physicalactivity/facts.htm#:~:text=Regular%20physical%20activity%20can%20help

Prasad, E. (2022). Guided meditations. *Mindfulness for Teens.* https://www.mindfulnessforteens.com/guided-meditations

Radhika Gupta [@iRadhikaGupta]. (2018, July 21). *Tweets* [Twitter profile]. Twitter https://twitter.com/iRadhikaGupta/status/10207016 41094324224

Raypole, C. (2020, May 19). Toxic friendship: 24 signs, effects, and tips. *Healthline.* https://www.healthline.com/health/toxic-friendships

Redbubble [@Redbubble] (n.d.). *Pinterest.* Retrieved February 4, 2023, from https://www.pinterest.ca/pin/35114072077974766/

Rice, C. (2022, November 14). Leadership quote of the week. *Laidlaw Scholars.* https://laidlawscholars.network/posts/we-need-to-move-beyond-the-idea

Rihanna (n.d.). Rihanna quotes. *BrainyQuote.* Retrieved February 4, 2023, from https://www.brainyquote.com/quotes/rihanna_7915 54

Ross, E. . (n.d.). Top 25 quotes by Ellis Ross (of 67). *A-Z Quotes.* Retrieved February 4, 2023, from https://www.azquotes.com/author/12659-Tracee_Ellis_Ross

Santilli, M. (2019, December 14). Would you ever throw your child a period party for their first cycle? Because that's a thing now. *Women's Health*. https://www.womenshealthmag.com/health/a30138 483/period-party/

Savage, J. (2015, October 30). Understanding your teen's attitude and body language. *Focus on the Family*. https://www.focusonthefamily.com/parenting/teen-attitudes-and-body-language/

Sleep in middle and high school students.. (2020, September 10). *CDC Healthy Schools*. https://www.cdc.gov/healthyschools/features/stude nts-sleep.htm#:~:text=Importance%20of%20Sleep

Smith, A. (2010, June 16). 7 signs that you're in a toxic friendship. *Psychology Today*. https://www.psychologytoday.com/ca/blog/healthy-connections/201006/7-signs-youre-in-toxic-friendship

Taylor, K. (2019, June 23). Nothing ever goes away until it teaches us what we need to know. *Kelli Taylor*. https://www.lifeaskellitaylor.com/meditation/nothin g-ever-goes-away-until-it-teaches-us-what-we-need-to-know

10 tips to boost your mental health. (2018, October 4). *BC Mental Health & Substance Use Services*.

http://www.bcmhsus.ca/about/news-stories/stories/10-tips-to-boost-your-mental-health

Tips for better sleep. (2022, September 13). *Centers for Disease Control and Prevention.* https://www.cdc.gov/sleep/about_sleep/sleep_hygiene.html

Trauma and shock. (2021). *American Psychological Association.* . https://www.apa.org/topics/trauma

Venkat, S. (2022, May 23). Health benefits of hobbies. *WebMD.* https://www.webmd.com/balance/health-benefits-of-hobbies

Walling, P. T. (2000). Consciousness: a brief review of the riddle. *Proceedings (Baylor University. Medical Center), 13(4), 376–378.* https://www.ncbi.nlm.nih.gov/pmc/articles/PMC1312236/#:~:text=Neuroscientists%20believe%20that%2C%20in%20humans

WebMD Editorial Contributors. (2022, August 28). Girls and puberty. *WebMD.* https://teens.webmd.com/facts-about-puberty-girls

Willard, C. (2020, June 11). Mindfulness for kids. *Mindful.* https://www.mindful.org/mindfulness-for-kids/

World Health Organization (WHO). (2021a, October 12). Stress. *WHO.* https://www.who.int/news-room/questions-and-answers/item/stress#:~:text=Stress%20can%20be%20defined%20as

World Health Organization (WHO). (2021b, November 17). Adolescent mental health. *WHO.* https://www.who.int/news-room/fact-sheets/detail/adolescent-mental-health

Your menstrual cycle. (2017, July 12). *Office on Women's Health.* https://www.womenshealth.gov/menstrual-cycle/your-menstrual-cycle#:~:text=Menstruation%20is%20a%20woman

Cover Image

Made in United States
Troutdale, OR
11/21/2024

25161664R00105